# Raising Kids God's Way

# Raising Kids God's Way

## A Biblical Guide for Christian Parents

## Kathi Hudson

CROSSWAY BOOKS • WHEATON, ILLINOIS
A DIVISION OF GOOD NEWS PUBLISHERS

*Raising Kids God's Way*

Copyright © 1995 by NACE/CEE

Published by Crossway Books
        a division of Good News Publishers
        1300 Crescent Street
        Wheaton, Illinois 60187

Cover photos: Jim Whitmer Photography, Wheaton, Illinois

Cover design: Cindy Kiple

First printing, 1995

Printed in the United States of America

Scripture taken from the HOLY BIBLE: NEW INTERNATIONAL VERSION®. Copyright © 1973, 1978, 1984 by International Bible Society. Used by permission of Zondervan Publishing House. All rights reserved.

The "NIV" and "New International Version" trademarks are registered in the United States Patent and Trademark Office by International Bible Society. Use of either trademark requires the permission of International Bible Society.

A small portion of the materials in this book were adapted from the seminar *Charting Your Family's Course*, developed and presented by Citizens for Excellence in Education (copyright © 1988 by NACE/CEE). For information on having this seminar presented in your church, please contact CEE, P.O. Box 3200, Costa Mesa, CA 92628 or call (714) 251-9333.

**Library of Congress Cataloging-in-Publication Data**
Hudson, Kathi.
    Raising kids God's way : a biblical guide for Christian parents / Kathi Hudson.
       p.    cm.
    1. Child rearing—Religious aspects—Christianity.  2. Child rearing—Biblical teaching.  I. Title
BV4529.H825 1995      248.8'45—dc20         95-15379
ISBN 0-89107-846-0

| 03 | | 02 | | 01 | | 00 | | | | | | | | | | |
|----|----|----|----|----|----|----|----|----|----|----|----|----|----|----|----|
| 15 | 14 | 13 | 12 | 11 | 10 | 9 | 8 | 7 | 6 | 5 | 4 | 3 | 2 | | |

*This book is dedicated to Bob and Jacki Simonds, my parents, who trained me up in the way of the Lord daily and through weekly Family Nights. Thanks, Mom and Dad, for "praying me through" the times when I tried my own way instead of God's.*

*And to my wonderful husband, Tim, for his patient support and input while I wrote this book.*

# TABLE OF CONTENTS

# FOREWORD
## By Dr. Robert L. Simonds

Christian parents today find themselves in the most demanding job in the history of man: how can we raise our children to live the Christian lifestyle?

Our world is constantly changing, exposing most children to unprecedented immorality, New-Age occultic religions, sex, drugs, gangs, atheism, social evils, and anti-family and anti-parent curricula in our public schools and media.

What can parents do? It seems almost impossible to know how to protect our darling, beautiful children from the evil pariahs of our society. Be encouraged, dear parents! You are holding in your hands one of the most important books you will ever read on raising your child. That's a big statement! Can it be true? Yes. Here is why.

This book is *not* a guide from a psychologist, nor any other "ologist." It is a clear compilation of Scripture—straight from our Lord's precious Book of Life, *the Bible.*

Kathi Hudson has searched the Bible for the directions God has given by commandment, example, parable, and teaching. It is God's plan! That's why the first of the four sections is titled, "A Sure-fire Plan." Not any man's plan—only God's plan. His plan is perfect! It cannot—repeat, *cannot*—fail. It really is a *sure-fire plan.*

It has been my great joy to raise five children by God's scriptural plan for His Christian families. As I read this book, I realized how many struggles I could have avoided by just reading and applying the Scriptures and precepts shared in this remarkable book.

It took me all of my life to search the Bible for these God-given teachings. You don't need to spend years compiling this material from God's Word. It's all collected and categorized here for easy reference.

You are about to take one of the most important journeys of your life—and the most practical and useful.

You will learn the difference between *teaching* a child and *training* a child. And with everything you teach, a method of training is suggested. By establishing a Family Night in your home, you will supply much of the *training* your children *must* have to be on automatic pilot in the Christian lifestyle.

The real goal of parents is to raise each child from birth to age eighteen, when many leave home for college, and to *know* in their hearts that their children will walk with God. That parental *peace* is our legacy from God. If you have total peace when your child goes off to college, you have succeeded! You've done your part. God will do His.

The best part about following God's plan as your children grow up is that you, as a parent, can enjoy every minute you have with them. Problems will be at a minimum, and joy will be at a maximum. Isn't that our best hope in life? God bless you and your precious little ones!

*Robert L. Simonds, Th.D.*
*President, NACE/CEE (National Association for Christian*
*Educators / Citizens for Excellence in Education)*
*1994*

# SECTION
## I

••••••••••••••••••••••••••••

# A Sure-fire
# Plan

———

◆

# CHAPTER 1

◆

# *Putting Your Kids on Auto-pilot*

Whether a high school student pressures your son to share a beer after school, how would you like your son to respond? When a friend tries to convince your child to cheat on a test, what will he or she do? When an older boy tries to seduce your daughter to have sex with him, what will she say? If your fourth-grader found a ten-dollar bill lying on the playground, what would he do with it?

If you're anything like me, and most Christian parents, you're very concerned about these answers. We'd all like to think our children will respond properly, based on God's standards of right and wrong. But how can we be sure of our children's character when we're not around? Wouldn't it be great if we could put them on auto-pilot so they'd automatically respond to the temptation of sin in a godly manner?

As parents, we *can* have the assurance that our *children* will be successful and that our *efforts* will be successful, if we follow the Lord's plan for training up our children in the way they should go (see Prov. 22:6). Remember, this verse has a *promise* attached to it. If I train my child up in the way he should go, God says that "when he is old he will not turn from it." Does this mean my child will never make a poor choice? No. Does it mean he'll never sin? No. Unfortunately, we are all born with a sinful nature, and none of us will ever achieve perfection by our own efforts, no matter how hard we try. But this promise from God means that youthful stumbles and mistakes will not get the best of my child. If he's properly trained to have a godly character, when he is old he **will** keep his faith.

We'd all like to insure that our children will secure that promise, and the first portion of the verse puts the condition on us; as parents we must properly *train* our children. The better job we do at training, the more straight a path our children are likely to walk on their way to becoming all that God wants them to be.

It is through proper training and teaching our children to make good decisions, to communicate with us, and to cling to the Lord that we can put our children on auto-pilot.

It is not enough to *know* how God wants us to live and who He wants us to be. We must practice (train in) what He teaches us until that becomes *who we are*. This is the process for developing our own character—character that determines who we are when no one else is around. We can use this same process to develop character in our children—character that will determine their automatic responses.

## THE DISTINCTION BETWEEN TRAINING AND TEACHING

The auto-pilot concept comes from my own father, Robert L. Simonds. You may have heard of him since he's a well-known national speaker to Christian parents on public school issues. He tells this story:

> Since World War II, I've been a trained commercial pilot with an instrument rating. Because of my good training and extensive experience, I could sit a young, 21-year-old man in a classroom and *teach* him: FAA and Naval Regulations; navigation; aircraft ordinance; mechanical indoctrination and radio procedures. He could pass all the examinations just fine. He would have had good conscientious teaching.
>
> However, if I were to put him in a new jet fighter plane, pat him on the helmet and say, "Have a nice flight, son," what would happen? It is likely he would crash and burn before he ever got off the runway. Why? He had good teaching but NO TRAINING.
>
> *Training* always involves *teaching*, but teaching seldom includes training. Teaching with actual flight training would have saved the young pilot's life and the $15 million fighter plane. Training would insure him of a good future in flying. So it is with our children. They need for us to follow God's plan of training.
>
> To train this young man, I would take him on flights where I piloted, so I could model proper procedure. Then I would fly with him—giving him some independence but being there to offer advice and han-

dle emergencies. Through this process, he would learn how to make important decisions, gain experience and have complete control of his flight.

Only after a great deal of practice in the air would he be trained for a solo flight. Then, as situations arose he would *automatically respond* properly, because of his extensive practical training. He'd be on human auto-pilot. He would automatically do the right thing, from good training.

You can see from this example that a lot more than teaching goes into training. This truth especially applies to parenting.

## The Game Plan

First, we must take stock of our present situation and make sure our foundation is secure. This involves clarifying our identity as children of the Lord and maximizing family communication.

Second, we must define our goal: training our children to be successful. So we must define success (or see how God defines success, since our desire as a Christian family is to be righteous and holy—to please God).

Once our goal is defined, we can examine the practicalities of training. This process involves prayer, modeling, teaching, encouraging, disciplining, and practice in all of life's areas.

This book takes a unique, practical approach to raising a godly, Christian family. And I can guarantee it works. Yes, that's a pretty big claim to make; but I trust in the Lord, and this book is based on scriptural principles. He created us, He put His children in our care, and we can be confident that His instruction works!

My personal advice to you on how to train your children is of no value, since you have no proof I'm right. But we know for certain that God's advice to you works. So this book is a compilation of Scripture that offers you a sure-fire plan.

In addition to exploring God's Word, we'll look at some practical ways to apply those scriptural principles to your family (to use them in training). Of course, what works best for you may differ from what works best for the Joneses or the Smiths. This practical advice is based on what has worked for others and is gleaned from the principles laid out in the Word of God. Though the practical application may differ somewhat from family to family, the principles remain the same.

## KEEPING YOUR CHILDREN ON GOD'S PATH

My own godly parents did an excellent job of training me. And I know their biblical method worked, because I am living proof. I "turned out!" And I see the same in my siblings. My mom and dad followed God's advice. Sure, I was a normal teenager. I've never been perfect. I've made mistakes, and I've fallen. But after a few years of "trying my own way," I came to stand firmly on my faith, with *both feet* on the narrow path to heaven.

Many children, if not most, go through a time of rebelling to some degree. They take a step or two off the path to see what's on the other side. But those, like me, who have been firmly grounded in the faith, trained to know right from wrong and do what is right and placed on auto-pilot, don't stray too far before they realize the sickness of sin and the beauty of living in Christ.

Children who have been firmly trained never really leave the Lord behind; He walks with us even through the valleys. The Holy Spirit is always reminding us of what is right and what is wrong. God is always reaching out to us with His love and forgiveness. And we recognize and feel His presence, because through our parental training we've been sensitized to the leading of the Holy Spirit, and we've been taught to make good decisions. Even when we make wrong choices, at least we know they are wrong! Realizing our error is the first step toward correction.

The *National & International Religion Report* (May 3, 1993) carried the results of a survey that illustrates this point:

> Children raised in consistently Christian homes are more likely to keep the faith in later years, says a recent study on apostasy. Sociologists Merlin Brinkerhoff and Marlene Mackie polled social science students at the University of Calgary and the University of Nebraska in the mid-1980's, and found that young adults were more likely to retain their early religious beliefs if they attended church at age 10 and did not experience their first religious doubts until their late-teen years. The more regular the church attendance, and the later the doubts came, the more persistent their beliefs. The groups most likely to retain the religious upbringing of their youth were Catholics and conservative Protestants.

Note that the children raised in *consistent* Christian homes, from denominations that place high value on training, were more likely to keep their faith. Virtually all of us must go through a time of questioning, whether mild and brief or long and severe, when we decide to make our faith *our own*, not just that by which our parents raised us. According to the Bible, and as evidenced by this study, solid, consistent, and thorough training will lessen that time of questioning and will bring the child to·personally-held convictions about his or her relationship with Christ.

The practical ideas on training used in this book come in part from a seminar called *Charting Your Family's Course*. This seminar was developed by Citizens for Excellence in Education, the Christian ministry in which I serve as vice president. The material from this seminar was developed with the help of many professionals—including educators, a principal, a Christian child psychologist, a pastor, and parents.

In addition to scriptural guidance and practical application for you as a parent, this book offers a clear way for you to open lines of communication and share what you are learning with your children, through a weekly Family Night. Family Night will be explained in further detail in Chapter 2. At the end of each chapter you will find discussion questions and activities to do, as a family, each week, to help you apply the practical Scripture lessons you are covering in this book. Family Night brings everything together and personally applies it to your family; thus these sections are called "Bringing It Home."

I hope you enjoy this book and find it to be practical and helpful. Certainly, training our children is not easy. However, as training becomes a reality, in the form of living the Christian lifestyle, raising our children can become pure joy. Our children are truly life's greatest pleasure. I hope you'll join with me in accepting the challenge. Cultivating a successful, godly family takes time, but it's an *investment* that will yield results in the lives of you and your children—eternal results!

# SECTION
# II

••••••••••••••••••••••••••

# Laying the
# Foundation

———

◆

# CHAPTER 2

♦

# *Family Night: Bringing It Home*

This book is specially designed to provide you with a fun, practical way of communicating with, teaching, and training your children. Of course, we must practice these three elements of parenting—communicating, teaching, and training—every day, in every moment of our lives. But it is helpful to have one designated night a week in which to focus on growing as a family and *training* our children. We must set aside time to do this.

The Christian lifestyle is an ongoing, constant, daily process, as is training our children. That is why it is important and helpful to have a special time set aside each week on Sunday mornings when we gather as a church and grow together. In the same way, we can use our weekly Family Night to gather and grow as a family. The weekly anticipation of such an event helps us keep our focus.

As I was growing up, I always looked forward to our Family Night. It was a special time of family discussion, prayer, learning— and fun playing together as a family. I always knew that no matter how hectic things got during the rest of the week, Monday night (the actual night varied over time) was a peaceful, relaxing time when we had the full, undivided, and unstressed attention of our parents.

Now that my brother, sister, and I are grown, we are all very close as a family, and I truly believe this is due in large part to the emphasis my parents put on Family Night. Some of my favorite memories growing up are of Family Night activities.

I will pass this legacy on to my own children, and you can too! It's very easy to do, and the payoff is tremendous! It just takes commitment to setting aside one night each week when the entire family makes it a priority to be together.

In this chapter I will explain the benefits and practicalities of holding a weekly Family Night. Then, in all succeeding chapters of this book, you will find a portion called "Bringing It Home." The discussion questions and Scripture studies found there are intended to be plugged into the generic Family Night format you'll find in this chapter. You may wish to select a fun family activity that ties into the lesson, but any activity that promotes family unity is appropriate.

## WHY HAVE A FAMILY NIGHT?

I believe Family Night is the key to tying the entire family together in the pursuit of family happiness and success in church, school, and home life. It can actually integrate Christ's teaching with school learning and family unity and caring. *Church, home, and school*—that's our field of training!

We've all seen the tragic decline in family values and devotion in this country. This trend has immeasurably weakened the family structure. How can we keep our family from becoming another statistic? By making our home life a major unifying nucleus and catalyst to all other activities.

Talking about this and even believing in this central fact of our Christian faith will not make it happen. *We must have a plan*, and we must dedicate our very being to its successful implementation in our home. This can literally transform a family into the supportive, loving environment God has intended for families to be.

The *purposes* of Family Night are:

- To *promote* family unity and love.
- To *instruct* the family in Christ's *truth* and to grow together in *faith*.
- To *encourage* communication within the family.
- To *pray* and rejoice together.
- To *integrate* biblical principles learned at church with school and home life; to enable us to live our faith in a practical manner.
- To *develop* a truly Christian spirit of love, yielding our individual rights as servants to one another.

- To *fellowship* together and *have fun* as a family.
- To *instill* in each member a desire to grow closer to the Lord.

Committing to this special quality time together can benefit your family, no matter what the ages of your children. The Bible says, "I love them that love me; and those that seek me early shall find me" (Prov. 8:17, KJV). No child is too young, or too old, to seek the Lord. Lessons should be adjusted to fit the learning levels of the various family members.

In fact, you can even start Family Night before you *have* children! My husband and I have made it a part of our relationship ever since we got married. Sunday has always been our "family day"—even just for the two of us. We set aside special time to study the Word together, learn together, communicate, and relax. It greatly enriches a marriage as much as a family! So it's never too soon to start.

I have several things that I want Family Night to accomplish within my family. I'm sure you have some goals of your own. You may find it helpful to jot down your personal family goals and discuss them at your first Family Night meeting, so that the children understand the importance and purpose of this special time. Here are a few of my own family goals, to help you get started in your thinking:

1. Learn from the Lord how we should live.
2. Discover the joy in committing ourselves to one another for life and in being a servant to others.
3. Share our joys and disappointments together in loving support.
4. Train ourselves in the discipline of the Gospel imperative for our lives and develop a godly lifestyle.
5. Model to our children how much Mom and Dad respect each other, and learn as a family from our mistakes.
6. Build our children's confidence in the Word and the church in an open, honest, and realistic way.
7. Learn how to deal with problems as part of our normal growth as persons. Hold one another accountable—in love.
8. Make school education a shared family experience, with certain expectations and much help and support.
9. Create a climate for open communication, where our children can share problems and questions honestly and we can learn their feelings, experiences, and views on life.
10. Encourage one another, and grow closer as a family.

## STRUCTURING YOUR FAMILY NIGHT

Family Night will be slightly different from family to family, based on your needs, the ages of your children, and your time constraints.

*When?* Hold a family meeting to choose a night that is convenient for all family members. Everyone must make a *firm commitment* to be there. Consistency is the key; so Family Night should be held on the same night each week. If your church doesn't have a Sunday evening service, that may be a good night for you to consider. For some families, a weeknight is best. Keep in mind that no night will be perfect for every person in the family; but the rewards of Family Night outweigh the sacrifice.

*What time?* Each family must choose the time best for them, but 6–9 P.M. is a good suggestion. Families with younger children will want to end earlier and cover a shorter time span. The main idea is to be consistent and punctual each week.

*Where?* Anywhere! The living room is usually convenient. Occasionally you may wish to hold your Family Night in a special place. It's always fun to worship the Lord together around a campfire at the beach or in the desert, or to marvel at His creations as you discuss the evening's lesson under the stars while sitting in a field or on a mountain. Look for opportunities for variety!

*Who?* Every member of the family needs to participate. It is especially important that the parents make every effort to be there, to show by example that they consider their family their top priority.

The following format works well for many people. You can decide how much time to spend in each portion of Family Night—prayer, discussion, activity, etc. I've found it helpful to be flexible. On some nights an issue may come up that needs more extensive discussion. Or there may be a need in the family that requires dedicated prayer. I would suggest this eight-step process:

1. *Start promptly at the designated time.* Have everyone gather in one room, each bringing their own Bible.
2. *Open with prayer.* For the opening, it's usually best for *one person* to pray (usually Dad).
3. *Share the reading of the Scripture lesson.* Take turns among all those who are able to read. A pre-reading child can participate by describing the pictures in his children's picture Bible.
4. *Discuss the relevance of the passage to your lives today.* This can

be facilitated by Dad and Mom asking thought-provoking questions. Encourage everyone to participate.

5. *Spend some time learning together.* Discuss an issue happening at school, a current event, or a good book. (See suggestions on learning activities later in this chapter.)

6. *Have a time of open communication.* Share family matters, and discuss any conflicts. Family members should share any specific prayer requests they may have. Encourage everyone to participate. You'll be amazed at what you learn about your children! Being open with them offers a good example and encourages them to be honest with you. This is a great time to discuss family and individual goals, plans, and successes.

7. *Pray and worship together as a family.* Each person can pray in turn or spontaneously. Everyone should have the opportunity to participate. I think a special feeling of family closeness is created when everyone sits in a circle and holds hands during prayer. Kneeling is also special. You may wish to close with songs of praise (even if you aren't famous for your singing voice!). Singing together creates a special bond.

8. Finally, *adjourn to a fun activity like a game or an outside event.* Choose an activity that everyone can participate in and enjoy. Remember, the key is *interaction*; so it's not a time to watch a TV program or a video! Try to leave at least one hour for this portion.

## SUGGESTED SCRIPTURE LESSONS

This book provides Scripture lessons, following each chapter, to get you started. After you have completed the book, you'll want to continue holding Family Night each week. You can find a wealth of Scripture lessons in any concordance (possibly even in the back of your Bible) by looking under topics of interest to your family, or even under the heading *Family.* As your children ask questions during the week, you can jot down ideas and address those issues with a Scripture lesson during Family Night.

For your convenience, here are a few more selected topical studies that you can use after you've completed the "Bringing It Home" lessons at the end of each chapter in this book. You'll have plenty of lessons to keep you going for at least a year.

## Promises to Children

Reverent children (Deut. 5:16); security in God (Ps. 27:10); seek early (Prov. 8:17); learn to obey God (Prov. 8:32); obey parents (Eph. 6:1-2; Prov. 1:8).

## References on Children

Prov. 6:21; 30:17; Ex. 20:12; Prov. 23:22; Matt 15:4; Deut. 27:16; Lev. 19:3; 1 Tim. 5:1.

## References on Home Religion and Instruction

Josh. 24:15; Job 1:5; John 4:53; Acts 16:15; 16:33; 1 Tim. 5:4.

## Topical Studies for Children

1. Who made the world? Gen. 1:1—2:3.
2. The woman who gave her home away for an apple: Gen. 3:1-6.
3. The voyage of the big boat: Gen. 6:14-22; 7:1-24.
4. The boy who sold his heritage and future for a meal: Gen. 25:29-34.
5. The boy slave who became prime minister: Gen. 37:13-36; 39:20-23; 41:1-44.
6. A baby's cry that got him a home in a palace: Ex. 2:1-10.
7. Moses' fit of anger: Num. 20:10-12; Deut. 3:23-26.
8. A band that captured a city by marching around it thirteen times: Josh. 6:1-20.
9. Gideon's search for God's will: Judg. 6:36-40.
10. The boy who could hear God's voice: 1 Sam. 3:1-21.
11. David, the giant killer: 1 Sam. 17.
12. The prophet fed by the birds: 1 Kings 17:1-6.
13. The chariot of fire: 2 Kings 2:9-11.
14. A race for a little boy's life: 2 Kings 4:18-36.
15. The ax that floated: 2 Kings 6:1-7.
16. An eating and drinking contest won by four young non-drinkers: Dan. 1:3-15.
17. Three boys who would not compromise: Dan. 3:1-30.
18. Three "fish" stories: Jonah 1–2; Luke 5:4-8; John 21:4-11.
19. The star that led to the baby's cradle: Matt. 2:1-11.
20. Five girls locked out in the cold: Matt. 25:1-13.
21. The boy who ran away from home: Luke 15:11-24.
22. The boy whose lunch fed 5,000 men: John 6:5-13.

23. The fatal lie: Acts 5:1-10.
24. The song that opened the jail doors: Acts 16:16-28.

## *Character Traits*

1. Humble: 1 Pet. 5:5; Phil. 2:3-4.
2. Loving: 1 Thess. 4:9; 1 Cor. 13.
3. Meek: Matt. 5:5.
4. Merciful: Matt. 5:7.
5. Obedient: Rom. 16:19.
6. Pure: Matt. 5:8.
7. Sincere: 2 Cor. 1:12.
8. Zealous: Titus 2:14.
9. Courteous: 1 Pet. 3:8.
10. Unity of mind: Rom. 15:5-7.
11. Hospitable: 1 Pet. 4:9.
12. Generous: 2 Cor. 8:1-7.
13. Peaceable: Heb. 12:14.
14. Patient: Jas. 5:7-8.
15. Content: Heb. 13:5.
16. Steadfast: 1 Cor. 15:58.

## SUGGESTED LEARNING EXERCISES

There are many educational exercises in which our families can participate. The few listed here are simply given as guidelines and to spur your thinking. These exercises should be geared to the interests of your own unique family and the subjects your children are learning, or not learning, in school.

- *Memory verses*: Family members may choose verses or passages from the Bible that they feel are particularly relevant to their life and circumstances at this time. Each one should memorize their chosen verse and recite it to the family at the next Family Night.
- *Share new knowledge*: Family members can share newly acquired knowledge with the rest of the family, such as an interesting fact they learned in school, an insight they had during a Sunday school lesson, or a new song they learned at a youth group meeting.
- *Books of the Bible*: You may want to have your family systematically memorize the order of the books of the Bible. To make this exercise even more meaningful, family members could give mini-

reports on various books (i.e., information on the author, the setting, the main theme, or the audience for which it was written).

- *Plan a lesson*: Older children might enjoy planning a lesson for the next Family Night meeting. They should be assigned (or choose) a specific topic or passage and be given any assistance they may require. The person preparing the lesson usually learns far more than the people hearing it!

- *Make covenants with one another*: These promises (whether to work on specific behavior or to help with a project) can literally change a family. If each person makes one covenant, this exercise will be most effective. Be sure to follow up on the covenants at the next Family Night to see if they were carried out as planned.

- *Secret Servant or Secret Encourager*: Draw names from a hat, so that each family member has the name of another. Keep the names secret! Then during the week each person should do something special for the person whose name they drew—either an encouragement (like a card or Scripture message) or a service (do one of their chores or be especially helpful in a secret way). Reveal the names at your next Family Night!

- *Prayer notebook*: Keep a notebook listing all the prayer requests your family makes at prayer time. Be sure to check the requests each week and record any answer. Remember, God answers prayer in three ways—"yes," "no," and "later"; but He always answers! The family's awareness of the power of prayer will increase, and this exercise will serve as an opening to explain the importance of faith and trusting in God when he says "no" or "later." He always knows what is best for us.

- *The literate American*: Your family may wish to use a controversial book by E. D. Hirsch, Jr. (*Cultural Literacy*) or another like it. Hirsch's book is said to describe "what every American needs to know" (academically). In briefing the vast knowledge pool needed to be an educated American, the author lists sixty-three pages of key words that any educated person should be able to explain. It is a great challenge to gradually wade through them. Your family may find it challenging to discuss five or ten word meanings at a time. Using an encyclopedia and dictionary is very helpful.

- *Reading together*: You may like to select a book by a good Christian author on a subject of interest to the entire family or read a piece of classical literature aloud for fifteen minutes a week. One book especially suited to Family Night learning is *Escape from Sugarloaf*

*Mine.* It takes three typical "values clarification" games and weaves them together with Bible stories, so children can learn how Christ addresses these values questions in contrast to the way the world does (for example, in public schools). (This is available for $7.00 only from CEE. We loved it! See the back page of this book for ordering information.)

## SUGGESTED ACTIVITIES

The number of different activities available to your family is truly endless. We have included a few ideas to stimulate your thinking.

1. Trivial Pursuit, Scrabble, and Pictionary are fun. These stimulating games also come in junior versions. Trivial Pursuit is especially a good educational tool.
2. Bible games are available at most Christian bookstores in a wide variety, all of which increase scriptural knowledge and interest in Bible study.
3. Playing charades with Bible stories is great fun.
4. Concentration is a card game in which all cards are laid out, facedown, and players take turns lifting two cards at a time, trying to remember pairs so they can be matched on a later turn. This is an excellent memory exercise.
5. Monopoly is an old favorite. It lasts too long sometimes, but it provides a lot of fun while teaching evaluation, negotiation, and economics.
6. Everyone can participate in making jam, applesauce, or canned goods.
7. Make homemade ice cream and then hold a family "stories and jokes" session as you eat it.
8. If you live near the woods, you could take a nature hike or go fishing.
9. Bowling and miniature golf are activities many families enjoy.
10. Going to a basketball, baseball, or other sporting event as a family is an option.
11. Attend a local city council or school board meeting that is discussing an issue important to the family. This teaches civic responsibility and participatory government.
12. Attend a cultural event such as an opera, a symphony, a ballet, or a musical.

13. Have a family sing. This allows children to play instruments and sing.
14. Have the kids put on a puppet show. They love this.
15. Think of activities especially available in your geographical area. For example, if you live near the sea, go to a grunion run. These little fish come to the shore by the thousands. They are a marvel to see.

## SPECIAL TIPS TO REMEMBER

Here are a few things we've found helpful to keep in mind so we can maximize our family time together and make Family Night a positive, anticipated experience for each member of the family.

**F** *FUN:* Family night should be a fun time—not a chore. It is a time of learning, sharing, and growing.

**A** *ACTIVITY:* Have an activity everyone can be involved in. Make sure it's fun *and* a learning experience whenever possible.

**M** *MANNERS:* Never allow family sharing to make anyone angry. Be sensitive to one another's feelings. Encourage openness with caring love.

**I** *IMAGINATION:* Use your imagination to come up with interesting, new ideas for activities and lessons that encourage all family members to get involved.

**L** *LEARNING:* Make each session a learning experience. Here's your opportunity for training.

**Y** *YEARNING:* Remember, our first priority is to instill a yearning for God and a desire to live our lives 100 percent for Christ!

### Bringing It Home

Here is a "generic" Family Night plan that you can use anytime. It is helpful to cover these Scripture, discussion, and application items briefly at each Family Night session to "bring home" the pastor's lesson from church the prior Sunday. (Mom or Dad will want to take a few notes during church to have on hand for this exercise. Or if the children don't hear the sermon because they are in Children's Church or Sunday school, you may want to gear the evening to that instead.)

| | |
|---|---|
| **Opening:** | What was the theme of the pastor's message (or the lesson in Children's Church or Sunday school) last Sunday? (Discuss it among the family.) |
| **Scripture:** | What Scripture did he use as his main passage? (Someone read it.) |
| **Discussion:** | What were his main points? (Discuss.) |
| **Learning Activity:** | Use your imagination to reinforce the pastor's main point by doing a creative learning activity (i.e., skits, drawings, games). |
| **Application:** | How can we apply the pastor's message to our lives individually and as a family? |

1. Have each person tell one way he or she will apply the lesson.
2. How can each child apply it to what he or she is learning at school this week?
3. As a family, how can we apply this lesson?

# CHAPTER 3

♦

# *Setting the Tone for Success*

Have you ever walked into a classroom where students were quietly working on a math assignment, asking the teacher for help as they needed it? Or working together in a group, cooperatively tackling a science project? When I walk into a classroom environment like that, I feel good inside. You can just *feel* the learning taking place.

Contrast that with memories from your childhood of the day you had a substitute teacher. Many substitute teachers maintain a successful classroom environment, but the students usually do all they can to make it difficult. Remember? When a substitute came, the other kids regarded it as a "play day," a time to see what they could get away with. Once in a while the class would get completely out of control—chaotic talking and shouting, paper airplanes, water fights in the drinking fountain—you get the picture. Remember those days of tormenting the poor substitute teacher?

Was any learning taking place in the chaos described above? Not likely. What a vast contrast to the first classroom environment I described! You can see what a tremendous impact the tone of children's surroundings, set by the teacher, has on the quality of learning and on how successful students will be.

Homes are very much like classrooms. Mom and Dad are the teachers and their offspring the students in the learning experience called *Life*. As the leaders of the household, parents set the tone. Every home environment is uniquely suited to the lifestyles, personalities, and needs of the family members. In the Bible we find some guidelines for our family environment:

> *And now this word to all of you: You should be like one big happy family, full of sympathy toward each other, loving one another with tender hearts and humble minds. Don't repay evil for evil. Don't snap back at those who say unkind things about you. Instead, pray for God's help for them, for we are to be kind to others, and God will bless us for it.*
> (1 PET. 3:8-9, TLB)

Peter mentions several specific elements that are present in a happy family—elements that create a successful home environment:

- *Sympathy*, which the *New World Dictionary* defines as "agreement in qualities; harmony; accord . . . a mutual liking or understanding arising from sameness of feeling."
- *Loving each other.*
- *Tender hearts*, or gentleness and tenderness without barriers.
- *Humble minds*, thinking of others' needs and desires above your own, without pride; servanthood.
- *Not seeking revenge* for wrongs done to you.
- *Not snapping back* when you are spoken to roughly or unkindly.
- *Praying for each other*, even when the person has hurt your feelings or done you wrong.
- *Being kind to others*; then God will bless you!

Note that Peter says that we "should be like" this happy family. Does this describe your family? Most of us must admit we have at least a few more things to work on. I know that when I'm very tired and frustrated, I'm more likely to snap back at my husband if he unintentionally offends me than I am to go to the Lord in prayer. I need to work on that. And I want to, because I know the tremendous difference it makes in my own home environment. One unkind comment, or even just a negative tone of voice, can create tension in the house for the rest of the day—even if it is quickly followed by a sincere apology.

Wouldn't it be great to have this kind of tone in our families? As parents, we set the tone for the entire family by the actions and attitudes we model. Think of your children and the typical responses, attitudes, and actions you see in their lives—both positive and negative.

This will give you a good starting point to examine whether you, as a parent, exhibit those same behaviors.

Next, decide what type of behaviors you'd ideally like to see in your children. Do you model those attitudes and actions around them?

The tone we set in our family invariably spreads outwards from our home. We've all heard the illustration of the father who got chewed out at work and came home and yelled at his wife, who in turn spanked the son, who then kicked the dog. Our actions spread. Our negativity rubs off on those we live with—anger, sadness, pain, and frustration. The good news is, so do our positive behaviors! When we as parents are happy, upbeat, encouraging, and full of joy, our children are more likely to exhibit those qualities and share them outside the home.

Our family tone affects the atmosphere at our place of work, and also the environment of our children's playtime. The attitudes and actions that we and our children have toward others begins in our *own home*. In Peter's advice to be a happy family, he is speaking to a church. Churches should have the same successful atmosphere that our homes have. This effort begins in the home of each family in the church, eventually spreading from the physical family to the larger church family. It starts with you and me! And we *can* do it, with God's help!

## THE IMPORTANCE OF TIME

Time priorities dramatically affect the course and feelings of our families. One study of 2,400 fifth-graders found that the one thing they said they found *most* upsetting was that they didn't get to spend enough time with their parents.

Children need both quantity and quality time—as much as you have to give. Finding enough time and the energy to really make it quality time is never easy. Nearly all of us are busy and overcommitted. It really comes down to a question of priorities. Is time with my child a priority? This may mean letting go of some other activities. Few good things happen by accident.

> *Any enterprise is built by wise planning, becomes strong through common sense, and profits wonderfully by keeping abreast of the facts.*
> (PROV. 24:3-4, TLB)

As parents, our primary enterprise is that of building our family. Successful family living takes planning. Throughout this book you will find strategies for *planning* your family's success. For these strategies to work, we must make time with our families a top priority. Having Family Night once a week is a great start toward dedicated quality time. But even that is not enough. A parent's job never ends; we are always modeling, instructing, and training our children by the very way we live our own lives. This is where quantity of time comes in.

Three basic tools will help you spend time that counts with your children—time spent in:

- Conversation.
- Questions.
- Reading together.

In *The Disadvantaged Child and the Learning Process*, Martin Deutsch found that in homes where conversation, questioning, and reading do not take place, a child asks fewer questions, uses shorter questions, and has both a smaller vocabulary and a shorter attention span. Practicing these activities at home will help your child achieve at school and in life.

Children grow up so fast. All parents occasionally feel they have failed their child or have not "been there"—that they have not been listening and attentive or even physically present when their child needed them. Rather than utter words of despair—"if only" ("if only I had taken the time," "if only I had listened"), we can use words of opportunity when these situations occur, saying, "Next time I'll go to her game" or "Next time I'll put down the paper and listen to him."

## TIPS ON COMMUNICATING

Family communication is key to creating a successful family environment. Two kinds of communication are vital:

- *Communication between the parents*: This is a key factor in successful families! *Consistency* is vitally important, as we will discuss later; so parents will want to discuss potential situations, rules, discipline, family goals, etc., ahead of time, in private. Any conflict of ideas between the parents should be resolved in private, then enforced with the children in unity.

  Family *security* is important to a child's sense of safety and wellbeing. Feeling secure frees the child to explore and learn in a safe environment. The best way to help your children feel secure is to have a strong marriage and to let them see your love and unity of mind and spirit.

- *Communication with the children*: The best way to know what goes on in your child's mind, how he or she feels, what she's learning at school, and what kinds of beliefs and attitudes she is developing is to keep open channels of communication. You'll want to do this with each child individually as well as within the family as a whole.

Three main elements encourage quality communication:

- Allowing time.
- Listening.
- Sharing openly.

*Timing* and *atmosphere* can affect how successfully communication will occur. Be sure to provide ample time for spontaneous discussion, where communication is natural and easy-flowing.

When I was growing up, my family always ate breakfast and dinner together. Some of my happiest memories are of these mealtimes. My memories aren't all specific, but they are filled with laughter and free-flowing discussion and storytelling. My dad is a natural storyteller, and I've always loved hearing about all the exciting things he's done in his life, from stories about World War II to exciting adventures he's had while flying missionary supplies to Mexico. While my mom doesn't have a storyteller personality, I've enjoyed and learned so much from stimulating discussions about politics, community issues, our family history, and travel destinations.

And don't forget family memories! Those special moments are kept alive for generations through remembering them together. Mealtimes are wonderful for this type of interaction. Families have busy schedules these days, but if you can at least make time for one consistent meal together each day you'll enjoy some fabulous times of open communication!

If you're like most parents, you probably spend a great deal of time in the car with your child—chauffeuring him or her from one activity to another. This undistracted time (especially if the radio is off) provides frequent special moments to just talk and listen to one another. And when you drive an entire group of your child's friends, you are afforded the chance to observe the type of peers your child has chosen to be close to, what issues concern them (what they talk about), and how your child interacts socially.

Family Night is another great opportunity for communication. Spontaneous and easygoing chatter usually accompanies the activity, while more serious topics can be broached during the discussion period. (See Chapter 2 for format and ideas.)

As Christians, we often get very busy with church work and helping others. Christ calls us to such service, and it should be an important part of our lives. However, we must be careful that it doesn't take place at the expense of our family. God has entrusted us with the custodial care of His children, and it is our primary duty to raise them and train them in the way of the Lord. Therefore, family time (and Family Night) must be a priority in our lives.

*Listening* is one of the most important, yet least practiced parts of communication. We can all improve our listening skills by carefully paying attention to the other person in a quiet, unhurried manner. If we listen to our children without interrupting, without thinking about what we're going to say next, and without jumping in to offer advice or judge them, we are really telling our children, by our actions, that they are important.

It's hard for some of us to be good listeners! I know that's one skill I've had to work at developing, since it doesn't come naturally to me. But it's worth the effort. If our children know that we are really listening and truly trying to understand rather than jump to conclusions, they'll be more likely to share their deepest concerns with us and make us part of their lives—which is what we all want, right?

Beyond listening to your child's words, be sure to notice his or her body language. Does he feel comfortable sharing with you, or does he need extra encouragement? Does he *appear* more anxious and frightened than he sounds? Your child will also, naturally, be observing *your* body language to see if you really are interested in what he has to say. If you keep looking at the clock or tapping your foot, you'll convey disinterest and your child will be less likely to share his feelings with you the next time.

When responding to your child, let him know you really care. Choose your words carefully so they sound thoughtful rather than like a lecture. You may wish to begin a sentence with "I am very concerned about . . ." or "I understand that it is sometimes difficult . . ." rather than with "You should . . .". If you're not sure you understand what

your child is trying to say, ask questions or repeat what you do understand and ask for confirmation.

Sometimes your child is not asking for advice, just for you to listen. By watching his feedback when you respond, you can tell if this
is one of those times. Maybe he just needs a hug and to know you care.

Finally, if your child tells you something you don't want to hear,
the temptation is to ignore it. But he could be alerting you to a potential problem; so further discussion is important.

Sharing our own experiences—even those we'd rather forget—can
save our children a lot of heartache of their own and can be a great
encouragement to them. Deuteronomy 4:9 says:

*Only be careful, and watch yourselves closely so that you do not forget
the things your eyes have seen or let them slip from your heart as long
as you live. Teach them to your children and to their children after them.*

The Bible instructs parents to *openly share* what they have learned
from their life experiences, so their children will benefit from the
lessons they've endured. Don't be afraid to show that you're human,
that you have sinned. We all have. We must let our children benefit
from our errors, by telling them our own experiences in learning the
*cost* of those sins. We can share the tough times as well as the good
times with them and talk about what the Lord has taught us through
our experiences.

It is so important that as parents we share with our children about
*God's work in our lives*. It is through hearing and seeing God work
that children build their own faith and that God becomes more real
to them.

I know a wonderful Christian family that has twelve children,
eight of them adopted. One of the birth children was recently sharing
with me the experiences she's had in seeing God faithfully and vividly
answer prayer. Her godly parents involve their children in praying for
guidance. They've prayed for the Lord to bring them special children
to adopt, they've prayed for a home large enough to house their family, and they've prayed for the opportunity to adopt additional children in order to keep siblings together.

As this girl was involved in family prayer for God's guidance in
these areas, she saw clear answers to prayer. This teenage daughter
recognizes the power and reality of God, and she is living her life com-

pletely for Him, thanks to the godly model her parents present as they openly share as God works in their family.

## DEVELOPING HOLINESS

A constant part of our Christian walk is to be transformed by the renewing of our minds (Rom. 12:2) and to be conformed to Christ's likeness (Rom. 8:29). This process develops our holiness as we remove the unclean from our lives and become filled with righteousness. Holiness refers to separation from sin, an absence of evil. I think we'd all like that in our homes! What should we be focusing on as our family develops in holiness, successfully becoming the kind of family God wants us to be?

> *Set your minds on things above, not on earthly things.*
> (COL. 3:2)

> *Therefore, as God's chosen people, holy and dearly loved, clothe your-selves with compassion, kindness, humility, gentleness and patience. Bear with each other and forgive whatever grievances you may have against one another. Forgive as the Lord forgave you. And over all these virtues put on love, which binds them all together in perfect unity.*
> (COL. 3:12-14)

Imagine what happy, loving households we all would have if everyone in them lived as God instructs in this passage. Notice that He doesn't say to do this "if you want to be happy" or "if you feel like it." He says it without qualifications—*just do it!* We are com-manded to teach our children to be holy and to have an attitude of love toward them. What a difference it will make in the *tone* of our homes if we follow this instruction!

Christ wants us to follow His example and put love above all else. We are to love our children the way the Father loves them and the way He loves us—unconditionally. Unconditional love easily forgives *and* forgets. We must love our children for *who* they are and because they are the children God gave us, not for what they *do*. The "love chap-ter"—1 Corinthians 13—bears special examination. This is God's model for love—the kind He has for us and the kind we should have for all others, including our spouse and our children.

There will be (and probably already have been) many times when our children don't resemble the image of this verse at all. Their action may be caused by a lack of training, modeling the behavior they see in us as parents, or by their carnal, rebellious nature coming out. This can be frustrating, but we must just recognize that the Christian life is a growth process, and God isn't finished with them yet. We can rejoice when they do model Christ and love them through the growing times, too.

## Bringing It Home

*Applying God's Principles: Please refer to Chapter 2 for ideas on Family Night format and activities.*

**Opening:** How would you describe the perfect family and the ideal home environment? How would you change our family if you could?

**Scripture:** Colossians 3:12-14.

**Discussion:** Identify and define each quality listed in the passage. On a scale of 1 to 10 (1 being totally absent, 10 being fully present), how would you rate our family on each of these qualities?

If Jesus were to visit our family, what would please Him the most about our behavior and attitudes? What would make Him sad? (Point out the fact that Jesus *is present* in our homes, always.) Read 1 Corinthians 2:16b (preferably in *The Living Bible*).

**Application:** 1. Have each person describe how they can contribute, individually, to improve on those behaviors and attitudes that make Jesus sad.

2. Have each person identify the quality listed in the Scripture passage that he or she finds most difficult to emulate, then discuss practical ways he or she can work on developing that quality this week (parents included).

# CHAPTER 4

◆

# *Our Identity in Christ*

Before we can begin the training process or set our goals, we must determine our present condition. As you can see from the previous chapter, a successful family lives a successful lifestyle—one that is positive, godly, and righteous. Each of us, as individual Christians, continually grow and become more Christlike as we continue to learn from the Word and apply it to our lives. Our lifestyle, and the fruit we produce, tells the world that we are Christians.

As parents, our own identity in Christ is of the utmost importance. If we wish to raise successful children, focused on the Lord, we must be able to model that behavior in ourselves.

*The righteous man leads a blameless life; blessed are his children after him.*
(PROV. 20:7)

We can start influencing our children for Christ before they are even born—by developing *ourselves* as godly models. Who I *am* speaks louder than what I *say*. My life, my life*style*, will be the message my child receives. So I must decide what I want that message to be. Personally, I want to convey total commitment to the Lord and to obeying His instructions and living in His will.

I'll never do this perfectly. No matter how hard I try, I can only become more Christlike and conform more closely to His image of perfection; however, I will never be exactly like Christ in this life, for He alone is perfect. But I will try to continue to develop holiness in my life by cultivating the qualities we have listed that characterize happy families.

While we are working on developing ourselves, we can also help our children develop a proper image of themselves in Christ. Without this foundational understanding of who we *are*, we cannot be a successful, godly family, for it is Christ who enables us to successfully serve Him, and it is our realization of our relationship to God that motivates us to obey.

Realizing who God is and what He's done for us by offering Jesus Christ as a sacrifice for our sins so that we might have eternal life gives us the faith to obey and the desire to conform to Christ's image. When we desire to become a godly model for our children, and when we wish for them to develop their character, we are setting forth on the path of being molded and shaped by the Holy Spirit.

How do we get the Holy Spirit to work in our lives? How do we know if He *is* working?

## KNOWING WE ARE SAVED

We are all sinful human beings. Romans 3:23 says, "For all have sinned and fall short of the glory of God." There is no way for us to get to heaven by our own actions—no way to earn eternal life with God. Because of God's great love for us (Rom. 5:8; John 3:16) and His immeasurable grace (unmerited favor), He sent his only son, Jesus Christ, to die on the cross for our sins and rise again three days later.

> *This righteousness from God comes through faith in Jesus Christ to all who believe. There is no difference, for all have sinned and fall short of the glory of God, and are justified freely by his grace through the redemption that came by Christ Jesus.*
> (ROM. 3:22-24)

> *For, "Everyone who calls on the name of the Lord will be saved."*
> (ROM. 10:13)

The natural consequence of sin is death (Rom. 6:23), but by God's grace we are saved by confessing our sins to the Lord and repenting of them (feeling sorry and determining not to do them again). If we believe and confess that Christ died for our sins and rose again to give us life, then we will be saved.

*That if you confess with your mouth, "Jesus is Lord," and believe in your heart that God raised him from the dead, you will be saved. For it is with your heart that you believe and are justified, and it is with your mouth that you confess and are saved.*

(ROM. 10:9-10)

The Holy Spirit works in our lives when we are saved, helping us conform ourselves to the image of Christ rather than the image of the world.

First John 2:3-6, TLB says:

*But how can we be sure that we belong to him? By looking within our-selves: are we really trying to do what he wants us to? Someone may say, "I am a Christian; I am on my way to heaven; I belong to Christ." But if he doesn't do what Christ tells him to, he is a liar. But those who do what Christ tells them to will learn to love God more and more. That is the way to know whether or not you are a Christian. Anyone who says he is a Christian should live as Christ did.*

*The character of even a child can be known by the way he acts— whether what he does is pure and right.*

(PROV. 20:11, TLB)

Your lifestyle will demonstrate whether or not you are a Christian. Your children will observe your actions and behaviors and know whether you are a Christian; they will develop an idea of what a Christian is, correct or false, based on your model. That's a heavy responsibility. How can we insure that we will continue to grow and live in Christ?

*Once you were alienated from God and were enemies in your minds because of your evil behavior. But now he has reconciled you by Christ's physical body through death to present you holy in his sight, without blemish and free from accusation—if you continue in your faith, estab-lished and firm, not moved from the hope held out in the gospel . . .*

(COL. 1:21-23)

*So then, just as you received Christ Jesus as Lord, continue to live in him, rooted and built up in him, strengthened in the faith as you were taught, and overflowing with thankfulness. See to it that no one takes you captive through hollow and deceptive philosophy, which depends on human tradition and the basic principles of this world rather than on Christ. For in Christ all the fullness of the Deity lives in bodily form, and you have been given fullness in Christ, who is the head over every power and authority.*

(COL. 2:6-10)

We must keep our faith strong and resist being deceived by the false philosophies of the world. We Christians must base our knowledge and behavior on the Word of God, being rooted and strengthened in our faith in Jesus Christ and the knowledge that He, through death, has made us holy in God's sight.

*Therefore, I urge you, brothers, in view of God's mercy, to offer your bodies as living sacrifices, holy and pleasing to God—which is your spiritual act of worship. Do not conform any longer to the pattern of this world, but be transformed by the renewing of your mind. Then you will be able to test and approve what God's will is—his good, pleasing and perfect will.*

(ROM. 12:1-2)

When we are saved, we are no longer of the world; we are transformed by the Holy Spirit, and then, as we walk the Christian walk, our character is continually being refined by the Holy Spirit's work in our lives. When we know what God teaches us, we can evaluate what the world says, and the Holy Spirit will help us discern right from wrong.

## A HEALTHY SELF-IMAGE

Our self-image should be based on this new identity we have in Christ. Proverbs 1:7 says, "The fear of the Lord is the beginning of knowledge." Wisdom begins with this basic understanding of who God is in relation to who we are. Recognizing His sovereign power over our lives makes us "fear" Him—to feel awe and reverence for His holiness and to desire to praise and worship Him because He alone is worthy.

On one hand, we are in awe of the Lord, full of reverence and appreciation for all He has given us—even eternal life—despite the fact that we are sinners and do not deserve it. We can never measure up to His standards on our own. We can never earn our way to heaven. But by His grace, God has saved us. This is an awesome truth to comprehend! And a very humbling one.

Balanced with this realization is the knowledge that each of us is very special; we are totally unique. God has a plan for each person's life, and He loves us unconditionally, no matter what we do. God has given each of us a unique personality, special talents and abilities that he wants to develop in us, and a special purpose for being on this earth. God knows us better than we could ever know ourselves.

*O Lord, you have searched me and you know me. You know when I sit and when I rise; you perceive my thoughts from afar. You discern my going out and my lying down; you are familiar with all my ways. Before a word is on my tongue you know it completely, O Lord.*
(Ps. 139:1-4)

*For you created my inmost being; you knit me together in my mother's womb. I praise you because I am fearfully and wonderfully made; your works are wonderful, I know that full well.*
(Ps. 139:13-14)

*All the days ordained for me were written in your book before one of them came to be.*
(Ps. 139:16)

One of the greatest gifts we can give our children is the understanding of who they are in Christ. God created your child in His image and redeemed her (or him) by offering her new life in Christ if only she will accept it. He has plans for her, knows everything about her, and is glorified when she reflects His qualities. She is His child— a member of the family of God!

## IS SELF-ESTEEM GODLY?

We hear so much about self-esteem these days. Almost every public-school classroom in the country has some sort of curriculum or effort directed at building your child's self-esteem. Should you be concerned about this movement, or is it important for your child to develop self-esteem?

Certainly it is vital that your child understand her (or his) identity in Christ. She is worthy because God has given her worth. God does not make mistakes. He created her perfectly, in His image, then valued her enough to send Jesus to die so that she might live. She is worthy because of Him!

But worth conveyed by the Lord is very humbling because there

47

is nothing we can do to be worthy ourselves. We are saved by grace—unmerited favor—and not because we are worthy. Because we are sinners, we are worthy only of death. It is only through Christ's worthiness and perfection that we are saved.

The Bible tells us:

*For by the grace given me I say to every one of you: Do not think of yourself more highly than you ought, but rather think of yourself with sober judgment, in accordance with the measure of faith God has given you.*

(ROM. 12:3)

Our own self-image must be constantly dependent upon our realization of and faith in all that Christ has done for us. We must compare ourselves only to Christ.

*Each one should test his own actions. Then he can take pride in himself, without comparing himself to somebody else, for each one should carry his own load.*

(GAL. 6:4-5)

We must test our own actions. We will always fall short of Christ's ideal, but we can see our growth toward it and can take pride in the Holy Spirit's work within us. We should never compare ourselves to others, since each person is growing in different areas as God has chosen, and ours is a heavenly standard by which to measure, not an earthly one. We can teach our children that their value and worth flows from what God has done. We have a divinely established worth based on God's esteem, God's worth, and God's image, not on our self-esteem, self-worth, or self-image.

It is important for us and for our children to have an accurate view or self-concept of our worth and value, to think neither too highly nor too lowly of ourselves, but to recognize who we are in Christ. Our worth or value does not come from achievement or possessions (a worldly standard) but from our relationship with God through Christ.

The world, and many public schools, teach "self-esteem" based on intrinsic self-worth. They teach your child to think of *himself* as his own god, 100 percent in control of his own life and destiny. This teaching is false and totally out of line with Scripture. You may have to counteract this teaching at home if your child is picking it up at school, from friends, or from television.

## GOD'S PURPOSE FOR US

Our children must understand that the Lord has a special purpose for them. God's purpose for each of us is:

- To be conformed to the image of God.
- To love and serve God.
- To be obedient to His commandments.
- To love and serve others.
- To be salt and light to the world.
- To bring godly influence to every aspect of life.

We must develop our abilities and talents because they are God's tools to enable us to live according to His purpose. By seeking and following God's plans for our own life and for our family, we will be successful.

> *"Be careful to obey all of these commandments. If you do what is right in the eyes of the Lord your God, all will go well with you and your children forever."*
> (DEUT. 12:28, TLB)

As our children develop their abilities and talents and use them to fulfill God's purpose in their lives, they will experience a sense of accomplishment and will build their confidence, which in turn will help them to be even more successful.

> *"For I know the plans I have for you," declares the Lord, "plans to prosper you and not to harm you, plans to give you hope and a future."*
> (JER. 29:11)

God has a special plan for your child. He wants him (or her) to succeed and has given him the talents and abilities to do so. Your child will probably never fully understand God's plan for him, and that's okay. We must have faith and trust God to work in our lives, leading us through those areas we don't understand.

> *Now we see but a poor reflection; then we shall see face to face. Now I know in part; then I shall know fully, even as I am fully known.*
> (1 COR. 13:12)

Our confidence is in God's knowledge and plan. He will enable us to succeed if we are sensitive to His leading and seek His will. It is not necessary for us to know and understand everything. If I waited to act until I had full confidence in myself, I would never accomplish anything. In fact, I wouldn't be a writer. But because I have confidence in God's abilities, I am able to step out in faith to fulfill the purpose He has for me.

As parents, we can help our children succeed by helping them develop their abilities and understand how to use them for the Lord, by instilling God's standards of right and wrong in our children's hearts, by encouraging our children to use the strength and confidence God has given them (Phil. 4:13), and by modeling our own faith, so that our children will have hope and will know their destiny (Col. 3:4).

Once our family has developed a healthy identity through our relationship with God, we will understand that He has a purpose for our lives. This realization fills us with an inner sense of well-being— the joy of knowing that God is in control and that He will enable us to succeed at what He has planned for us. This gives us the confidence to achieve success. In addition to experiencing this myself and as a family, I can help my children experience it personally as well.

## Bringing It Home

*Applying God's Principles: Please refer to Chapter 2 for ideas on Family Night format and activities.*

Opening:      How does God show you that He loves you? (Make sure each child understands that they can have life through Christ.)

Scripture:    Psalm 139:1-4, 13-16.

Discussion:   How well does God know you? Is there anything God doesn't know about you? How does He know you so well?

Does God have a plan for your life? How can you learn about what that plan is and follow it?

Knowing that God knows you intimately, better than you know yourself, that He is the ultimate power in your life and that He has a special plan just for you—how does that make you feel about yourself? Where does your image and worth come from?

**Application:**  1. We know how God shows His love for us. How do we show our love for Him? Make a list of ways that you can show God how much you love Him.

2. Each family member should choose one new way they can grow closer to the Lord and learn more about His plan for his or her life. Begin doing it right away. Here are some ways to do this:
   - Have a quiet time each day (pray and study the Scriptures).
   - Read the Bible each night.
   - Ask God to show you what to change in your life.
   - Learn memory verses each day or each week.

# SECTION
# III

◆◆◆◆◆◆◆◆◆◆◆◆◆◆◆◆◆◆◆◆◆◆◆◆◆

# Defining
# the Goal

◆

# CHAPTER 5

◆

# *A Tale of Two Men*

$T$*he First Man*: Once upon a time a child was born to godly parents. Even before the baby, named John, was born, God had an important mission for John's life. After he grew up, John did something a bit odd. He moved to the wilderness. He didn't look like a civilized person; he looked more like a wild mountain man or a hippie. He wore clothing woven from camel's hair and a leather belt. He ate strange food, too—wild honey and locusts (large grasshoppers). This man, John, had a tough message to preach. He told people to repent from their sins. He spoke of a Messiah coming to save the people. Many people laughed at him and ridiculed him. But John didn't let those people scare him away. He knew that he spoke the truth and that his purpose in life was to herald the upcoming arrival of Jesus. He obeyed God despite the persecution. Because of his obedience, many people came to listen to him, and they believed the truth he spoke. He baptized many people.

At this time there was a king named Herod. He married his brother's wife, Herodias. John had the courage to tell Herod and Herodias that their marriage was immoral in the sight of God. Because of this, he was thrown in jail and was eventually beheaded.

*The Second Man*: Once upon a time, long before the time of John, another boy was born. His name was Saul. Saul was born with many advantages. He was very rich (his father was a wealthy and influential man from the tribe of Benjamin). Saul was called "the most handsome man in Israel" (to put it in modern language), and he was large and muscular. He grew up to be a powerful man, and God appointed him to be the first king of Israel.

God gave Saul many opportunities, and when Saul obeyed God, he was blessed and conquered other armies. But Saul was impulsive and liked to rush ahead with his own plans without waiting for God. Sometimes he even specifically disobeyed God.

Because of Saul's disobedience, God decided to make David king instead of Saul. Saul pleaded for forgiveness; but it was too late, and David became the new king. Saul did not accept this as God's plan. Instead, he was very jealous and plotted to kill David, but he wasn't able to. Once, when he didn't know what to do, he asked a witch for advice. Eventually Saul died by his own hand on the battlefield.

## THE MORAL OF THESE STORIES

Which of these men was successful? Imagine that both of these men lived in today's world and their stories were taking place right now. From the world's point of view, John the Baptist would be seen as a religious fanatic, a complete nut. In fact, sadly, even many of today's Christians would think John was too extreme and would wonder if he had a screw loose.

On the other hand, Saul would be hailed as a success in the eyes of the world. He had "everything": looks, money, power, and influence. He was *king*. In fact, many would view David as the bad guy—the interloper—and would feel sorry for Saul's "bad luck."

How would you view these two men if you saw their stories in the news? Which one would your child consider a success?

What counts is *God's* opinion of these two men. Here's what Jesus himself had to say about John the Baptist:

> *When John's disciples had gone, Jesus began talking about him to the crowds. "When you went out into the barren wilderness to see John, what did you expect him to be like? Grass blowing in the wind? Or were you expecting to see a man dressed as a prince in a palace? Or a prophet of God? Yes, and he is more than just a prophet. For John is the man mentioned in the Scriptures—a messenger to precede me, to announce my coming, and prepare people to receive me. Truly, of all men ever born, none shines more brightly than John the Baptist."*
> (MATT. 11:7-11, TLB)

Jesus said that of *all the men ever born*, John shines the brightest!

That is pretty high praise, especially coming from God Himself! I would have to conclude that God considered John the Baptist a great success, even if the world did not.

But John came to a tragic demise, didn't he? He was beheaded! Hardly what we'd expect of a success! John knew that his life on this earth was but a speck in time. His reward did not come on this earth; it came in heaven. Success doesn't guarantee us an easy life or wealth. But it will bring us eternal rewards.

Saul, on the other hand, had the outward appearance of a man who "had everything"—a success in the eyes of the world. And God could have made him a great success. God chose Saul to be king, and God wanted to crown his efforts. Unfortunately, Saul had his own plans and his own ambitions. He refused to obey God.

> *Samuel replied, "Has the Lord as much pleasure in your burnt offerings and sacrifices as in your obedience? Obedience is far better than sacrifice. He is much more interested in your listening to him than in your offering the fat of rams to him. For rebellion is as bad as the sin of witchcraft, and stubbornness is as bad as worshipping idols. And now because you have rejected the word of Jehovah, he has rejected you from being king."*
> (1 SAM. 15:22-23, TLB)

Samuel had warned the people and their king, Saul, by saying:

> *"Now if you will fear and worship the Lord and listen to his commandments and not rebel against the Lord, and if both you and your king follow the Lord your God, then all will be well. But if you rebel against the Lord's commandments and refuse to listen to him, then his hand will be as heavy upon you as it was upon your ancestors."*
> (1 SAM. 12:14-15, TLB)

But Saul did not heed the warning. And when he lost everything, *then* he begged God's forgiveness. But he didn't change his life, for he continued to sin and jealously threatened David's life for many years. Time and again the Lord was sorry He'd ever made Saul king (see 1 Sam. 15:11, 35).

## THE REAL DIFFERENCE

There are countless examples of men like John and Saul who made a choice either to obey or disobey God, and those decisions determined whether or not their lives were successful. There are many men, like

Saul, whom God greatly wanted to use, and did use and bless at times, but who did not live up to their potential and truly have a successful life because their motivation was flawed.

In Matthew 7:24-27 (TLB) Jesus offers us a beautiful picture of how the results of our lives (our success or failure) depend on the foundation upon which our lives rest:

> "All who listen to my instructions and follow them are wise, like a man who builds his house on solid rock. Though the rain comes in torrents, and the floods rise and the storm winds beat against his house, it won't collapse, for it is built on rock. But those who hear my instructions and ignore them are foolish, like a man who builds his house on sand. For when the rains and floods come, and storm winds beat against his house, it will fall with a mighty crash."

As we examine the lives of Bible characters, we can determine what kind of foundation they built their lives upon. Did they succeed in obeying the Lord throughout their lives, or did their lives fall apart as they fell into sin?

It all boils down to motivation. Were they motivated by God, called by Him, and obedient to His plan—building their lives on the rock? Or were they motivated by their own desires, perhaps even *trying* to walk with the Lord but lacking commitment when His plans didn't coincide with their own earthly desires? Those who are driven by their *own* plans and ideas, their own definition of success rather than God's, will crumble because their life is built upon sand.

What is the motivation of our family? What kind of foundation do we build our lives upon?

We all want to be successful—eternally successful. And as parents, we want that for our children as well. If I could have one wish, it would be for my children to walk closely with the Lord and obey Him fully—no matter what earthly consequences that brings—because I know the *eternal* results of their success in this endeavor are what really matter. We're just travelers on this earth.

My greatest desire and strongest prayer is for my entire family, including myself and my husband, to be successful in God's eyes. I know that a key area where I must succeed is the training of my children to obey the Lord. The world models many false ideas of success; it is up to me to instill in my child *God's view of success.*

In the next couple of chapters we'll look more deeply into the Bible's insights on success, and I hope the Family Night exercises found under "Bringing It Home" will help you to lead your children to a godly view of success.

## Bringing It Home

*Applying God's Principles: Please refer to Chapter 2 for ideas on Family Night format and activities.*

**Opening:** Read the tales of the two men, the paraphrased stories of John the Baptist and Saul, contained in this chapter. Each family member should select the man they think was more successful and explain why.

**Scripture:** Genesis 37, 39-45 (especially note 39:23)—the story of Joseph. (For younger children, you may wish to read a shorter storybook version or to paraphrase the story. Older children will enjoy the entire passage.)

**Discussion:** Was Joseph successful in his life? Why? Discuss how God used Joseph, even through difficult trials. How did Joseph handle the temptation of Potiphar's wife?

**Application:** 1. If you went through the difficulties Joseph did—being thrown in the well, being imprisoned—what would your attitude be? Is God in control of such situations?

2. When things go wrong in your life (as they sometimes appeared to in Joseph's), does this mean you are failing?

3. How did Joseph treat his brothers after the terrible thing they did to him? How can you show love and forgiveness to someone you know?

4. Based on the reasons you found for Joseph's success in life, how can you also be a success in life?

# CHAPTER 6

◆

# *What Is Success?*

If I asked you to describe a successful person, what would you say? What is *your* definition of success? If I asked this question of a room full of twenty people, I'd get at least fifteen different answers. We all have our own vision of what *success* means.

Although the word means different things to different people, it is vitally important for each one of us to examine our view of success and the influences upon our lives that have formed that viewpoint. Our ideal, our goal for our own success, is based on a multitude of visual and verbal cues that we have received throughout our life—from television, books, our parents, friends and peers, famous personalities, church, the Bible, teachers, our culture, and more—all of which are filtered through our own wants, desires, and values to form our own personal vision of success.

Success is one of the most loaded concepts in our culture, because each of us strives to reach that ideal. What is the purpose of living, if not to be successful? Have you ever known anyone who *wanted* to be a failure in life?

I grew up in Orange County, California, where success is primarily measured in material wealth, power, and image. In fact, Orange County is one of the yuppie capitals of the country, where anyone who is anyone drives a BMW or Mercedes while conversing on their car phone to set up a power lunch. Just for the record, my family never had any of these things; we were very happily middle-class. But I grew up surrounded by a strong cultural statement that equates success with having a wealthy and powerful image.

I know a lot of people who adopted the Orange County view of success. They clearly believed that *image* is everything; you don't have to actually *have* money, just enough credit to *look* like you have money. Unfortunately, no one told these people that credit runs out and someday you have to pay the piper. At some point you must adjust your standard of living to what you can afford!

While some of these friends still buy into the image, others have decided that the nineties call for a more *meaningful* view of success than that of the materialistic eighties. While they struggle to pay their debts and hold on to their jobs in a tough economy, they are spending time, instead of money, on greater social concerns like the environment and politics. They're even getting "back to the family."

But is this a proper view of success? Certainly family values are vitally important and a top priority; so is doing good and helping others. But *why* are they doing it? Mostly because of social pressure; it's the "in" thing. They'll move on to something else when the next fad comes along. Perhaps it's also due in part to the realization that something is missing in their lives.

The town you live in may have a totally different culture than Orange County. In fact, I myself now live in a small farming community in central California, where the values are very different. I don't know if this town ever went through a materialistic phase, since I wasn't here. But most of my acquaintances here seem to view success as having a comfortable life, raising their family, and being involved with social causes.

Other friends of mine, particularly those in northern California, seem to view intellect as the key to success. They strive to be better than everyone else with their speaking and thinking skills and to impress the world with their cultural savvy. To them, success will come when they are widely recognized for their creative and intellectual pursuits.

Perhaps this is stereotyping. I don't mean to imply that everyone who lives in those geographical areas conforms to my generalizations. I am simply speaking of differences I have personally observed in my own friends and acquaintances in order to make the point that geography and culture greatly affect our view of success and that many different definitions exist by which to guide one's life. Most of these definitions hold success up as a goal to be achieved—something to reach at some point in life. And attainment is measured relative to the degree of worldly success that your peers have reached.

With all these versions of success, based on wealth, intellect, power, family, social involvement, etc., how are we to know what *success* really means? My personal concern is not how others define success; it is how God defines success and what God requires of me. My own measure of success is to one day hear my Lord say, "Well done, good and faithful servant."

## WHY SUCCESS MATTERS

It is important for us, as parents, to carefully define our own measure of success. If we don't, society will subconsciously do it for us. We are important models and teachers for our children, and one of our responsibilities is to help each of our children form a healthy, godly view of success. It is our definition of success that ultimately determines which paths we take in life, since we are always aiming at the goal of being successful.

In the last chapter we looked at examples of two lives covered in the Bible. One was a success, in God's eyes; the other was not. God *blessed* the efforts of John the Baptist because John obeyed Him and followed His guidelines for success. If we want God to bless our efforts, we too must follow His formula for success. The reward is great—blessing and contentment, not to mention eternal life with the Lord.

## A BIBLICAL VIEW OF SUCCESS

In 2 Chronicles 31:21 (KJV), the Bible tells us why King Hezekiah was a success:

> *And in every work that he began in the service of the house of God, and in the law, and in the commandments, to seek his God, he did it with all his heart, and prospered.*

In *everything* he did, Hezekiah was motivated by his love for the Lord and his desire to serve and obey God. As parents, we want the Lord to prosper our family, our children. We want the Lord's blessing on all that we do, and we pray for our children to be successful in the eyes of God. Psalm 1:3 (KJV) describes a successful man:

> *And he shall be like a tree planted by the rivers of water, that bringeth forth his fruit in his season; his leaf also shall not wither; and whatsoever he doeth shall prosper.*

From this biblical description, we can discover several key concepts.

- First, success involves *doing*. A successful life produces fruit and prospers in its works.
- Second, a successful person has *strength*, like a tree, with his or her feet firmly grounded. A tree is stable and lasting; so a successful person would have qualities of *consistency* and *perseverance* and will not wither. A successful person is *grounded in the Word*, rooted firmly on the rock of Christ's truth.
- Third, the fruit is brought forth *in God's timing*, in the season He has designated. A successful person must be walking in God's pathways and must be sensitive to the Holy Spirit's direction, so that he produces the correct fruit that is intended and does so in the season God ordains.

God gives each of us certain abilities and gifts that enable us to produce certain works, just as He designs an apple tree to produce apples and a peach tree to produce peaches. Therefore, we could define success as:

> Success is living in such a way that you are using what God has given you—your intellect, abilities, and energy—to reach the purpose that He intends for your life.

Your child has many God-given abilities—abilities to create, to build, to organize—in short, to achieve. But God intends each person to use his or her abilities differently to fit in with His perfect plan. That is why success must always be measured in relation to God's intention for each one of us, not in comparison to other people.

There is no single mold for a successful person, even in a biblical view. And there is no means for comparison with each other, because God has created each of us uniquely, and He has a special plan for each person's life. To be successful, we must obey and fit into His plan, using the unique gifts and abilities He's given us.

Success is personal and in relationship to God. It includes how I live each area of my life. A successful lifestyle is more important than having one particular area of achievement. It involves keeping a balance in the activities and achievements in my life, while using my God-given abilities. Success does not arrive in a moment; it is an ongoing process, a lifestyle.

We are called to "bloom where we are planted." In other words, God has placed each of us in life situations according to His will. We are to be satisfied and content in any situation and perform the work He has called us to do there.

> *Each one should remain in the situation which he was in when God called him.*
>
> (1 COR. 7:20)

When we live a successful lifestyle, we are good stewards over the things God has given us—our abilities, intellect, finances, creativity, etc.—and are meant to use them for His glory. Our goal is to become more Christlike, exhibiting the characteristics that He exhibited: for example, being holy in character, becoming a servant, and seeking God's will.

> *For God did not call us to be impure, but to live a holy life.*
>
> (1 THESS. 4:7)

As we obey and grow, our lifestyle becomes more successful. Success is an inner character discipline—a process of developing the qualities God has given us—not an external goal.

How many times have you heard the phrase, "living up to his potential"? It communicates a clear idea of achieving one's best. But it implies a point of success prior to which the child is a failure. Have you ever known someone to *"achieve* their potential"? I don't believe I've ever heard that said! It's always assumed that we can do more than we are currently doing—and generally we can.

Perhaps it is more realistic and uplifting, and more in line with the scriptural principle of living a successful lifestyle, for us to encourage our children to *make the most of their abilities,* try their best to live as God intends them to, and do His will. One godly woman I know has defined success as "getting in God's will early and staying that way."

## THE FRUIT OF A SUCCESSFUL LIFESTYLE

Success is lived in many forms, but the evidence is always a fruitful life. What does the Bible mean when it says God *prospered* successful men? Most of us think in monetary terms or in terms of luxury when we hear the term *prosper.* But God's blessings frequently don't involve riches.

*Success is evident in a holy, righteous life that bears fruit of eternal value.* Godly success is not measured in material terms. The ultimate success is to find favor in God's eyes—to hear Him say, when we stand before His throne, "Well done, good and faithful servant."

Sometimes God does reward us with material success as well—usually when He knows we will be good stewards of what He entrusts us with and will use it to bear further fruit. But a worldly measure of success should never be our goal. Pleasing the Lord should be our goal.

It is so easy for us to be fooled by worldly possessions and prosperity into thinking we are successful. But Christ tells us:

> *"What good will it be for a man if he gains the whole world, yet forfeits his soul? Or what can a man give in exchange for his soul?"*
> (MATT. 16:26)

The answer is, *nothing.* In fact, worldly prosperity can be difficult to overcome. In Matthew 19:24 Jesus says, "it is easier for a camel to go through the eye of a needle than for a rich man to enter the kingdom of God."

> *"You say, 'I am rich; I have acquired wealth and do not need a thing.' But you do not realize that you are wretched, pitiful, poor, blind and naked."*
> (REV. 3:17)

Pretty strong words to the rich! Is it wrong to have wealth? No. God has greatly blessed many of His servants with material riches, as the Bible clearly illustrates. What separates those who succeed from those who fail is their attitude *toward* the riches and the affect it has on their character.

> *Tell those who are rich not to be proud and not to trust in their money, which will soon be gone, but their pride and trust should be in the living God who always richly gives us all we need for our enjoyment. Tell them to use their money to do good. They should be rich in good works and should give happily to those in need, always being ready to share with others whatever God has given them. By doing this they will be storing up real treasure for themselves in heaven—it is the only safe investment for eternity! And they will be living a fruitful Christian life down here as well.*
> (1 TIM. 6:17-19, TLB)

Our prosperity as Christians, our riches, are intangible rather than monetary. The Lord provides for our needs and fills us with the contentment that comes from living in His will and serving Him.

*Do you want to be truly rich? You already are if you are happy and good. After all, we didn't bring any money with us when we came into this world, and we can't carry away a single penny when we die. So we should be well satisfied without money if we have enough food and clothing. But people who long to be rich soon begin to do all kinds of wrong things to get money, things that hurt them and make them evil-minded and finally send them to hell itself. For the love of money is the first step towards all kinds of sin. Some people have even turned away from God because of their love for it, and as a result have pierced themselves with many sorrows.*

(1 TIM. 6:6-10, TLB)

Obviously, having a lot of money and material wealth is not God's idea of success. In fact, it can be very dangerous. Yet, this is the dominant message of success our children receive from the world—especially from television. The above Scripture passage impresses upon us the importance of instilling a godly view of success within our children and helping them to put money in its proper place.

God desires for us to obey, live a holy life, and live with Him forever in paradise. The contentment that comes from knowing I am living in a way that pleases Him is my *earthly reward; heaven* is my eternal reward. We are blessed with peace, contentment, and happiness when we live a successful lifestyle. If I am in Christ's will, living a righteous life, what have I to fear? I know He has a plan for me and will care for me and will enable me to do what He intends. I believe there is no greater peace and security than this knowledge. *Freedom is a reward of successful living.*

*Be sure of this: The wicked will not go unpunished, but those who are righteous will go free.*

(PROV. 11:21)

*. . . I have learned the secret of being content in any and every situation, whether well fed or hungry, whether living in plenty or in want. I can do everything through him who gives me strength.*

(PHIL. 4:12-13)

What is happiness? Contentment. For many years I had a saying taped to my desk. I'm not sure where it came from, but it struck me;

so I copied it down. I looked at that saying many times a day for several years until it has become a basic philosophy of my life. And I believe it ties in well with what Paul has to say about contentment. The saying is this:

*Happiness is wanting what you have, not having what you want.*

Isn't that profound? So many people go through life thinking, "If only I had a new car, I would be happy." Once they get the car, they continue, "If only I had a new boat, I would be happy." It's just like getting a raise in pay. We always think that an extra hundred or two hundred dollars a month would be "just enough" to make us comfortable. But enough is never enough, is it? As soon as we get what we want, we remember we wanted something else, too.

Ingraining this simple little saying and Philippians 4:12-13 into my mind has literally changed my life—and my view of success. I used to view success as being happy. Really, I still do. But I used to think I would be happy "if only I had one more thing" or "if only I could do something else." Now I realize that my happiness lies totally in the knowledge that I am living in Christ's will.

The secret of being content is knowing that Christ is in charge of your life, and so you never have to worry! He has placed me in the exact circumstance in which I now find myself, good or bad. I am there for a reason—it's part of the plan; so I can be happy with what I have! This is a profound truth to teach our children, who are the most captivated victims of an advertising culture that says happiness is just around the corner with one more purchase!

Our greatest reward for living a successful lifestyle is the Lord—the peace that we have when we follow Him, knowing that He will guide us and tell us what to do. He is all we need. He is fully sufficient.

*The Lord himself is my inheritance, my prize. He is my food and drink, my highest joy! He guards all that is mine. He sees that I am given pleasant brooks and meadows as my share! What a wonderful inheritance! I will bless the Lord who counsels me; he gives me wisdom in the night. He tells me what to do. I am always thinking of the Lord; and because he is so near, I need never to stumble or to fall.*

(Ps. 16:5-8, TLB)

When our joy is in the Lord, we will be completely satisfied, happy, and even much healthier overall!

> *"Happy are those who long to be just and good, for they shall be completely satisfied."*
> (MATT. 5:6, TLB)

> *A cheerful heart is good medicine, but a crushed spirit dries up the bones.*
> (PROV. 17:22)

This special happiness that comes from the Lord is not the fleeting earthly happiness that we momentarily feel when someone brings us flowers or gives us a compliment. The Bible says in Proverbs 16:20, "blessed [happy] is he who trusts in the LORD." The Bible speaks of an inner happiness that goes beyond external circumstances—the kind of happiness that Paul could have in *any* situation! We can have that kind of happiness and peace, too, if we trust in the Lord!

## HOW TO HELP YOUR CHILD BE SUCCESSFUL

The greatest gift we can give to our children is to train them to be *really* successful, in God's eyes. By doing so, we will also be giving them the gift of happiness and contentment.

> *If they obey and serve him, they shall spend their days in prosperity, and their years in pleasures.*
> (JOB 36:11, KJV)

We must teach our children what the Bible has to say about success, so they don't fall prey to the deceptive thinking illustrated in Revelation 3:17, which I quoted earlier. They could literally lose their soul because of a false idea of success and riches and fail to enter heaven because of it—a chance we simply can't take.

All of society is teaching our children the *world's* idea of success and false values. Satan's trap is open wide. As a Christian parent, I may be my child's only chance to learn about the *Lord's* definition of success. The Bible says it is my duty to train my child to live a successful lifestyle and to obey Christ's commands. I want my child to be a light in the darkness of the world.

> *Do everything without complaining or arguing, so that you may become*
> *blameless and pure, children of God without fault in a crooked and*
> *depraved generation, in which you shine like stars in the universe as you*
> *hold out the word of life—in order that I may boast on the day of Christ*
> *that I did not run or labor for nothing.*
>
> (PHIL. 2:14-16)

One good way of helping your child to distinguish between godly success and worldly success is to teach them about the three *myths of success.*

- The first of these myths is the *myth of perfection*—the idea that success means you must always achieve perfectly. Consider Babe Ruth: in 1927 he hit sixty home runs, more than anyone in the history of baseball . . . But did you know that same year he also *struck out* more than anyone else in baseball? We should not focus on the number of times we fail, but rather on the number of times we *succeed*!

  In Philippians 3:12 we read, "Not that I have already obtained all this, or have already been made perfect, but I press on to take hold of that for which Christ Jesus took hold of me." Success involves *perseverance*, not perfection!
- The second is the *myth of finality*—believing that success is a point rather than a process. One achievement doesn't make me a success any more than one failure keeps me from being successful. It is our lifestyle that counts, not a certain point at which we must arrive. Philippians 3:14 says, "I press on toward the goal . . ." The effort to live a godly lifestyle is continuous. A successful lifestyle is much more important than a successful moment.
- Third is the *myth of comparison*—that success is measured by comparing ourselves to others. We can't compare ourselves to others because we are all *different* (Gal. 6:4-5). Different doesn't mean better or worse—just different! It's what makes you *you*! We are each a special and unique creation of God, and He has a special plan for each one of us.

We live a successful lifestyle as we listen to God and obey Him. The prophet Amos obeyed God, though the prophecy he was to deliver was a difficult one, not joyfully received by the people. He had no special qualifications for the task, just that he obeyed the Lord. That made him a success.

> *Amos answered Amaziah, "I was neither a prophet nor a prophet's son,*
> *but I was a shepherd, and I also took care of sycamore-fig trees. But the*
> *Lord took me from tending the flock and said to me, 'Go, prophesy to*
> *my people Israel.'"*
> (AMOS 7:14-15)

Sometimes when we think too highly or too lowly of our own abilities, we get in the way of God's plan for our life and may even miss an opportunity to serve Him and be successful. For example, Moses didn't want to lead the Israelites out of Egypt because he had a speech impediment and didn't feel he could speak and lead. Jonah was afraid of God's call to prophesy in Nineveh.

Despite their human doubts, God proved in both situations that He is able to use us for whatever He calls us to do. We need not compare ourselves to the apparent abilities of others who have served the Lord in a similar way, nor should we be deterred by our past failings. God has a special plan for each of us, and He will reveal it when the time is right. We must simply be ready to obey and do our best.

Look at the disciples. Would you have chosen them for such an important mission? God could see much more in them than we can. He can see a special use for each one of us too. He uses *human beings* to do His work, not superheroes.

> *Brothers, think of what you were when you were called. Not many of*
> *you were wise by human standards; not many were influential; not*
> *many were of noble birth. But God chose the foolish things of the world*
> *to shame the wise; God chose the weak things of the world to shame*
> *the strong. He chose the lowly things of this world and the despised*
> *things—and the things that are not—to nullify the things that are, so*
> *that no one may boast before him. It is because of him that you are in*
> *Christ Jesus, who has become for us wisdom from God—that is, our*
> *righteousness, holiness and redemption.*
> (1 COR. 1:26-30)

In training our children, we can help them understand that to be successful they must be *called (led)* by God according to His will, not driven by their own desires. When our hearts are readied, God's clear call is made known.

While encouraging our children in their uniqueness and abilities, it is also important to instill a good dose of *humility*. It is only because

God has *given* us our talents that we are able to use them. And only when we use them for Him will we be successful.

Humility is especially necessary to see us through those times when God uses us in His plan and we feel the thrill of that success. It's an awesome feeling to be used by God! One that can easily go to a person's head and invalidate him or her for future success, as we've seen with many characters in the Bible and modern-day evangelists. The "thrill of success" can especially be a threat when it comes in a way that the world also considers a symbol of success, like money or fame.

I like what Charles Spurgeon, a nineteenth-century English minister, had to say on the subject:

> Success can go to my head and will unless I remember that it is God who accomplishes the work, that he can continue to do so without my help, and that he will be able to make out with other means whenever he wants to cut me out. (Cited by J. Oswald Sanders, *Spiritual Leadership* [Chicago: Moody Press, 1967], p. 23)

We can teach our children humility without degrading their abilities or dampening their confidence if we gently use scriptural reminders that Christ enables them to serve Him and that all glory and honor belongs to Him. We can thank the Lord, with our children, for the opportunities He gives us to glorify Him.

> But "Let him who boasts boast in the Lord." For it is not the one who commends himself who is approved, but the man whom the Lord commends.
>
> (2 COR. 10:17-18)

> Before his downfall a man's heart is proud, but humility comes before honor.
>
> (PROV. 18:12)

Another way we can help our children to live a successful lifestyle is by helping them grow in character and righteousness. We can do this through modeling growth to them and helping them understand the kind of character traits God desires for us to build. These qualities will help them to live successfully.

> For this very reason, make every effort to add to your faith goodness; and to goodness, knowledge; and to knowledge, self-control; and to self-

*control, perseverance; and to perseverance, godliness; and to godliness,
brotherly kindness; and to brotherly kindness, love. For if you possess
these qualities in increasing measure, they will keep you from being inef-
fective and unproductive in your knowledge of our Lord Jesus Christ.
But if anyone does not have them, he is nearsighted and blind, and has
forgotten that he has been cleansed from his past sins. Therefore, my
brothers, be all the more eager to make your calling and election sure.
For if you do these things, you will never fall, and you will receive a rich
welcome into the eternal kingdom of our Lord and Savior Jesus Christ.*
(2 PET. 1:5-11)

Because Christ saved us, we desire to grow and become more
Christlike so He can use us. This passage of Scripture offers us a recipe
for success.

Success is a *process*, as this passage clearly illustrates. As we grow
in one area, we will add other areas, increasing our character. We
become more and more successful, in God's eyes, as we increasingly
obey Him, becoming more Christlike and righteous in our character.
This process is not just for adults—it's for children too!

Parents can encourage this growth in their children and can also
model a life that illustrates a constant growth process, a successful
lifestyle. As the character of each family member grows and becomes
more godly, the result will be:

- Increased effectiveness in the Lord's work.
- The blessing of living in God's will.
- An auto-pilot response that reflects Christ's nature and desires.
- A more harmonious and loving home.
- Protection from falling into sin.
- A rich welcome into heaven.

*Teaching*, if alone, ill equips a person for success, since the Bible
says knowledge is not enough, but is just one step on the ladder
toward becoming holy (a success in God's eyes).

"Knowledge" can be dangerous if it is not accompanied by "self-
control." Solomon is a perfect example. He was one of the wisest men
ever; yet he fell into sin because he lacked self-control. With knowledge alone, one may become puffed up. Self-control keeps the *balance*
between knowing who you are and who you are not.

To "self-control" we are told to add "perseverance"—a key ingredient of success, as we discussed earlier. In persevering, we keep on
doing good, obeying, no matter what happens.

The characteristics in this passage of Scripture paint the picture of servanthood, don't they? If we do these things, God will use us (our "calling" will be "sure"). If we choose not to do them (v. 9), we'll become as blind as an unbeliever and will lose our eternal perspective. As parents, we must help our children understand and choose the Lord's way.

The formula given here in 2 Peter ensures success. We're told that if we do these things, we'll never stumble or fall! That is a *promise*. We'll receive a "rich welcome" in heaven. What a wonderful assurance if we simply follow God's plan!

A step-by-step pattern for spiritual growth is provided in those seven verses. We can set goals to master each command, one at a time. Faith starts with reading the Word and *practicing* it. Then we are to add moral excellence (as modeled by Christ). We can increase our knowledge of God through studying and learning Scripture. Isn't it wonderful how the Lord gives us such specific biblical instruction? As we follow this plan for our own lives, we can also use it to train our children!

## Bringing It Home

*Applying God's Principles: Please refer to Chapter 2 for ideas on Family Night format and activities.*

**Opening:**  What does it mean to be happy? How can you become content? Is it possible to be happy and content in *any* situation?

**Scripture:**  Philippians 4:4-9, 11-13.

**Discussion:**  What should we do when we are afraid or anxious? What will God do to help us? Can we feel this peace and happiness always? Why? What kinds of things should we concentrate on thinking about? Can you do *anything*? What? How will doing these things help you to be successful?

**Application:**  1. Review the "Three Myths of Success" and have each child comment on he or she feels about these concepts.

2. Have each child describe how they would like to be successful and why this would make him or her happy.

3. Ask each person to select one character trait to work on this week that will get him or her started on a process of successful living (see 2 Pet. 1:5-11 for guidance and motivation).

# CHAPTER 7

◆

# *Prerequisites for Success*

Lf you asked your child to name five successful people, who would he or she name? Perhaps he would name the President of the United States, an athlete like Michael Jordan, or a singer like Whitney Houston. Whether we like it or not, our children look to public figures (whom they primarily observe on television) as models.

What do these public figures model? The world's image of success. While some of the models may be good people, most of them are not what we would consider suitable heroes whom our children should strive to be like.

As we train our children to view success from a godly point of view, and as we attempt to model a successful lifestyle in the best way that we can, we are helping our children to form more realistic and eternally-based views of success. It's also helpful to offer heroes who were successful in God's eyes for our children to model.

Some excellent choices include: Jesus, Paul, Joseph, Hezekiah, Daniel, Job, or Shadrach, Meshach, and Abednego (the three young men God delivered from the fiery furnace), just to name a few.

The Bible gives us clear and specific examples that illustrate why some people were successful while others were not. Let's examine these in a bit more detail and glean from them wisdom to pass on to our children—specific conditions for success and hindrances of which to beware.

## HINDRANCES TO SUCCESS

Before we look at specific recipes for success, let's remind ourselves of a few cautions. It's important to help our children understand that they must guard against these areas if they want to be
successful.

- *Unbelief* is a hindrance to success. Success comes when we believe
  the Lord, have faith in His sovereign power, and obey His Word.
  Without belief, one cannot have faith and one has no reason to
  believe.

> *Yet the promise remains and some get in—but not those who had the*
> *first chance, for they disobeyed God and failed to enter. . . . "Today*
> *when you hear him calling, do not harden your hearts against him."*
> (HEB. 4:6-7, TLB)

- *Satan* is another hindrance to success. He tries to tempt us to do
  evil, plagues us with doubt, and tries to discourage us by perse-
  cuting us.

I can relate to this hindrance very well. In our ministry to
Christian parents and teachers of public school children (Citizens for
Excellence in Education), we are lied about, persecuted, hated,
ridiculed, and mocked at every turn by the non-Christian education
establishment—simply because they feel threatened by God. If I did
not have total faith in the Lord and His power to overcome, I would
have given up long ago. But I do have faith, and time and time again
I have seen the Lord triumph against all earthly odds! Remember, He
who is in us (Christ) is greater than he (Satan) who is in the world (1
John 4:4)!

- *Laziness or lack of action* is another hindrance to success.

> *I went past the field of the sluggard, past the vineyard of the man who*
> *lacks judgment; thorns had come up everywhere, the ground was cov-*
> *ered with weeds, and the stone wall was in ruins. I applied my heart to*
> *what I observed and learned a lesson from what I saw: A little sleep, a*
> *little slumber, a little folding of the hands to rest—and poverty will come*
> *on you like a bandit and scarcity like an armed man.*
> (PROV. 24:30-34)

If we are not proactively living a life that pleases the Lord, all sorts
of "thorns" and problems will creep up on us. We will bear "weeds"

rather than fruit. This especially applies in training our children. If we do not actively train our children in the way of the Lord, the ruin of the world will be evident in their lives. Their roots will be in the training of the world rather than in the words of Christ, thus resulting in actions that are like thorns.

- *Lack of commitment* will also hinder success. When we look at Amaziah's life (2 Chron. 25), we see that much of the time Amaziah was successful and God blessed him. But, unfortunately, his commitment was not complete, and so he was open to a fall.

*He did what was right in the eyes of the LORD, but not wholeheartedly.*
(2 CHRON. 25:2)

Since his commitment wasn't *full*, wholehearted, there was room for temptation to take hold in Amaziah's life—and it did. He turned to the worship of false gods. So Amaziah's life ceased to be successful, and eventually he was killed.

*From the time that Amaziah turned away from following the LORD, they conspired against him. . . .*
(2 CHRON. 25:27)

Uzziah, Amaziah's son, was also successful *as long as he sought the Lord.* But just as Uzziah modeled his father's righteousness, he also left a gap in his commitment that eventually led to his downfall. His fame led to pride that led to his failure and eventual death by leprosy. What a sad commentary, but a powerful message to us: success *can* be removed, and we can fall, even after being used by God in a mighty way! Notice the impact parental modeling had on Uzziah:

*He [Uzziah] did what was right in the eyes of the Lord, just as his father Amaziah had done. He sought God during the days of Zechariah, who instructed him in the fear of God. As long as he sought the Lord, God gave him success.*
(2 CHRON. 26:4-5)

*But after Uzziah became powerful, his pride led to his downfall. He was unfaithful to the LORD his God.*
(2 CHRON. 26:16)

79

## CONDITIONS FOR SUCCESS

Now that we know what hindrances to avoid, let's look at some specific action to take so we can be successful! First, let's look at the Lord's instruction to Joshua:

> *"Be strong and very courageous. Be careful to obey all the law my servant Moses gave you; do not turn from it to the right or to the left, that you may be successful wherever you go. Do not let this Book of the Law depart from your mouth; meditate on it day and night, so that you may be careful to do everything written in it. Then you will be prosperous and successful. Have I not commanded you? Be strong and courageous. Do not be terrified; do not be discouraged, for the Lord your God will be with you wherever you go."*
> (JOSH. 1:7-9)

In His instructions to Joshua on how to be successful, God emphasized three points:

- Precise obedience.
- Knowledge of God's Word.
- Courage and strength.

Do you notice how these three important areas work together and feed one another? First of all, obedience is the key. God knew what must be done for Joshua's efforts to be a success; so he told Joshua to do exactly as he was instructed—"do not turn from it to the right or to the left."

- When God instructs us to obey, He means for us to obey His instructions precisely—not almost, not mostly, but exactly! And always! Just a slight deviation, turning "from it to the right or to the left" just *one degree*, doesn't seem like much and is easily justified. But if an airplane pilot is off course by just one degree when he takes off, he may land several hundred *miles* away from his intended destination! We must obey *exactly*.

The Lord also told Joshua to dwell on His Holy Word and meditate upon it day and night. It is necessary for us to know and understand God's Word in order to obey. Joshua was told to do this so that he "may be careful to do everything written in it." Notice the word "everything." That's a tall order, but it's what God asks of us. How can we obey everything if we haven't read His Word to find out what "everything" is? God knows what is best, always; we are not to pick and choose which parts of His instruction to obey.

Finally, God emphasizes the importance of Joshua's strength and courage. Certainly Joshua was facing a daunting challenge—bringing the Israelites into the Promised Land. After years of wandering in the desert, he was well aware of all that could go wrong, and he faced a frightening responsibility. But the Lord *commanded* him to have courage.

Where does this courage come from? When we follow the first two conditions for success, knowing and obeying the Word, we will have strength and courage. If we know the Word, we are well aware of God's awesome power and His perfect plan. This gives us *faith* that conquers fear. When we are living in obedience to Him, we can have assurance that He will take care of us; this contentment in every situation gives us *perseverance*.

Let's look at a few more verses to reinforce the importance of knowing and obeying God's Word and having faith to conquer fear and allow us to persevere and have courage. God clearly repeats the point that these are key ingredients for success!

> *Carefully follow the terms of this covenant, so that you may prosper in everything you do.*
> (DEUT. 29:9)

> *"Then you will have success if you are careful to observe the decrees and laws that the LORD gave Moses for Israel. Be strong and courageous. Do not be afraid or discouraged."*
> (1 CHRON. 22:13)

> *Despise God's Word and find yourself in trouble. Obey it and succeed.*
> (PROV. 13:13, TLB)

> *But the people that do know their God shall be strong, and do exploits.*
> (DAN. 11:32, KJV)

Note that success is *conditional*. Notice the first two verses, for example: "carefully follow . . . *so that* you may prosper"; "you will have success *if* . . ."

The Lord promises us that if we act according to His will and by His plan and instruction, we will succeed. If we do not wholeheartedly obey, we will fail.

The Bible illustrates a few more conditions to success. Let's look at them, to form a complete and precise recipe for success.

> *When the king realized how much the Lord was with David and how immensely popular he was with all the people, he became even more afraid of him, and grew to hate him more with every passing day. Whenever the Philistine army attacked, David was more successful against them than all the rest of Saul's officers. So David's name became very famous throughout the land.*
>
> (1 SAM. 18:28-30, TLB)

Why was David such a success while Saul was a failure? Because of one key difference: the Lord was with David, not Saul. The Lord is with us when we are acting for Him, according to His will, in obedience to Him. When He supports us, He will crown everything we do with success. So another key ingredient is to:

- Be in God's will.

God's support to make us succeed in our efforts is *conditional* upon our *action of obedience*. It's a cause-and-effect relationship, as we can see from these next two Scriptures. Living in obedience to the Lord will bring success.

> *In everything that he [Hezekiah] undertook in the service of God's temple and in obedience to the law and the commands, he sought his God and worked wholeheartedly. And so he prospered.*
>
> (2 CHRON. 31:21)

> *Hezekiah trusted in the LORD, the God of Israel. There was no one like him among all the kings of Judah, either before or after him. He held fast to the LORD and did not cease to follow him; he kept the commands the LORD had given Moses. And the LORD was with him; he was successful in whatever he undertook.*
>
> (2 KINGS 18:5-7)

We find three more conditions for success revealed in these verses that, again, tie in with our previously listed conditions:

- Action.
- Commitment.
- Faith.

In order to succeed, we must take action—active obedience and active effort to attain the other conditions. We see that Hezekiah *"sought"* his God and *"worked* wholeheartedly."* These words show action and effort on Hezekiah's part.

Hezekiah also showed full commitment; he worked *"whole-heartedly,"* holding nothing back. He *"held fast* to the LORD and *did not cease,"* illustrating full commitment to the Lord and perseverance. And he *"trusted* in the LORD"*; he had faith. Remember, it is this faith that enables us to have courage and to persevere! In doing these things, Hezekiah was blessed with great success.

Finally, the last ingredient for success, and one of the most important, is one that cuts to the core of everything we do. The question is, "Why am I doing it? What is my motive?"

> All a man's ways seem innocent to him, but motives are weighed by the LORD. Commit to the LORD whatever you do, and your plans will succeed. The LORD works out everything for his own ends—even the wicked for a day of disaster.
>
> (PROV. 16:2-4)

> In everything you do, put God first, and he will direct you and crown your efforts with success.
>
> (PROV. 3:6, TLB)

If we desire to be successful, our motive must be to put God first and to glorify Him. All we do must be done unto the Lord. Thus, the final ingredient for success is:

• Righteous motivation.

Doing a good thing isn't enough; we must be doing it for the right reasons. We've all seen the tragedy of ministry leaders who failed and fell because their motivation was not the Lord's glory but rather their own desires for wealth and power. These men (and women) may have been doing something that truly appeared to minister to people and was scripturally correct, but their heart's motivation was selfish.

The area of motivation is a particularly delicate one. God says, "All a man's ways seem innocent to him." Isn't that the truth! We humans have a tremendous ability to justify our actions, don't we? We even fool ourselves, and that's frightening! But we never fool the Lord. He knows our innermost motives, and He will judge our actions through the screen of our motives. God's will is always accomplished, despite the wrong motives of many who claim to serve Him. But those who are not putting God first and acting for His glory will not have successful lives.

In these two passages we are given a wonderful promise and an assurance of success. If we have the right motivation, putting God first in *everything* we do and committing our plans to the Lord, He *will* direct our efforts and crown them with success!

## THE KEYS TO SUCCESS

To summarize, the keys to success that we've uncovered in the Bible are:

- Courage and strength.
- Precise obedience.
- Knowledge of God's Word.
- Being in God's will.
- Action.
- Commitment.
- Faith.
- Righteous motivation.

We can use these keys to success to specifically train our children in how to live successfully and accomplish right goals in their lives. We are only successful when our goals are in line with God's will.

Here are some basic rules to attaining goals. When children are taught these basic scriptural truths and trained by the model of their parents and Bible heroes, they will be equipped for success.

1. *Put God first.*

"But seek first his kingdom and his righteousness, and all these things will be given to you as well."
(MATT. 6:33-34)

2. *Obey God's instructions* (read the Bible to know them).

Do not merely listen to the word, and so deceive yourselves. Do what it says. Anyone who listens to the word but does not do what it says is like a man who looks at his face in a mirror and, after looking at himself, goes away and immediately forgets what he looks like. But the man who looks intently into the perfect law that gives freedom, and contin-

*ues to do this, not forgetting what he has heard, but doing it—he will be blessed in what he does.*

(JAS. 1:22-25)

3. *Act towards achievement of the goal* (have faith).

*Brothers, I do not consider myself yet to have taken hold of it. But one thing I do: Forgetting what is behind and straining toward what is ahead, I press on toward the goal to win the prize for which God has called me heavenward in Christ Jesus.*

(PHIL. 3:13-14)

4. *Persevere with courage—never give up.*

*Let us not become weary in doing good, for at the proper time we will reap a harvest if we do not give up.*

(GAL. 6:9)

Be consistent and fully committed!

5. *Have the proper motivation: Christ!*

*I eagerly expect and hope that I will in no way be ashamed, but will have sufficient courage so that now as always Christ will be exalted in my body, whether by life or by death. For to me, to live is Christ and to die is gain.*

(PHIL. 1:20-21)

## MODELING JESUS

Of course, Jesus is the best model of success, and He is the best model for our children. Sometimes we look at all God asks of us and we think, "Obey everything? I just can't do it." That's one of the reasons Jesus came to earth as a man, lived as a man (though also fully God), and faced temptation just as we do. Through it all He persevered and had unwavering faith and a servant's attitude.

Jesus exhibited all the qualities we've listed as keys to success. His courage and strength are unmatched. His motivation and ability to live in God's will were above reproach. He knew the Word, and He lived it, obeying the Heavenly Father even though He was also Himself God.

> *And even though Jesus was God's Son, he had to learn from experience*
> *what it was like to obey, when obeying meant suffering. It was after he*
> *had proved himself perfect in this experience that Jesus became the*
> *Giver of eternal salvation to all those who obey him.*
>
> (HEB. 5:8-9, TLB)

According to John 10:17-18, Jesus voluntarily *chose* to die for us. He *chose* to obey God even though it meant terrible suffering. He can give us the strength to obey *every* command.

Parents can train up their child well, but ultimately the child must still make the choice to obey and fully commit to serving the Lord, just as Jesus had to choose. If the child is not trained up in the ways of the Lord, his chances of making the right choice are lessened.

In order to obey, we must *know* God's laws—by reading and studying (meditating upon) His Word. There is also a condition: we must *act* upon that knowledge and live in accordance with God's will. Training our children to know God and live a righteous, holy life is the key to their true future success!

We can help our children choose a successful, godly lifestyle by training them to have the proper focus, obey and act, persevere, and have the proper motivation.

## *Bringing It Home*

*Applying God's Principles: Please refer to Chapter 2 for ideas on Family Night format and activities.*

**Opening:** Name five successful people or five of your heroes. What makes them so successful?

**Scripture:** Psalm 1:1-3.

**Discussion:** What does it mean to be "blessed" and to "prosper"? If you want to be successful, what does this passage say you should do? What does it say you should not do?

**Application:** Review the keys to success and the basic rules for attaining goals listed at the end of this chapter.

1. Discuss any terms that aren't fully understood by everyone.

2. Each person in the family should decide which of the keys to success are present in his or her life and

which are still needed. What must he or she do to make any missing keys part of his or her life, to enable him or her to live successfully?

3. How did Jesus model each of the basic rules for attaining goals? Was He successful? How can you model Jesus in your daily life?

# SECTION
# IV

◆◆◆◆◆◆◆◆◆◆◆◆◆◆◆◆◆◆◆◆◆◆◆◆

# Training
# Your Child

◆

# CHAPTER 8

◆

# *How to Train Your Child Successfully*

Now that we've evaluated our current position and defined our goal (success), we're ready to begin the actual training process.

We're all familiar with Proverbs 22:6—

*Train a child in the way he should go, and when he is old he will not turn from it.*

Remember the automatic pilot concept we discussed in the first chapter? Well, that's the purpose for training. Through the various components of training, we will be setting our children up to succeed—instilling in them the godly character that will enable them to make good decisions and automatically respond to life situations in a way that pleases the Lord. We will thus put our children on auto-pilot and give them the best possible chance of making good choices and determining to serve the Lord.

We must never forget that every child has a different personality, and all have the freedom to choose whether or not to follow the Lord. Some will go through a period of exploring the "other side" of life before they firmly commit to the Lord. But the Bible promises that if we train them up in the way of the Lord, when they are old they will not depart from it. Eventually, if their character is rooted in righteousness, our children will find their way back to the roots of their faith.

## TURNING THE CONCEPT INTO A PLAN

We're often exhorted to train our children, but we're seldom given precise instructions on how to do that. Of course, there is no "one and only" way to train a child. What feels comfortable for you may differ from methods others prefer. But the basic components are all the same; and since they are taken from scriptural principles, we can be assured that they work! The rest of this book will focus on those basic principles and will offer practical ideas on how to put them into practice at home. I'm sure you'll come up with many more excellent ideas of your own.

You may be thinking, "This sounds pretty complex. How long is it going to take?" Well, I won't lie to you. You can't just sit down and train your child over dinner, or even in one long intensive training day. Training takes place over time—from birth on—and until the child reaches maturity, for sure!

Every parent is training their child, whether they realize it or not. Some are training their children in the way of the Lord, others in the way of the world. But training is most effective when it's a conscious, well-planned effort.

We all hope that our children will emulate only what we do right and not notice our mistakes. As parents, we're famous for wanting our offspring to "Do as I say, not as I do." Unfortunately, training doesn't work that way. Children see us and model us as we really are; so we must first mold ourselves into the type of godly person we want our children to be. Good training is a regimen based on a plan; it's not an occasional effort that takes place when we feel inspired. *Teaching* our children (what we *say*) can take place sporadically or be fit into a schedule. But *training* (what we *do*) is constant and ongoing. That's one key difference between training and teaching. Teaching is just one component of training.

Training involves at least five major elements:

- Praying.
- Modeling.
- Teaching.
- Encouraging.
- Disciplining.

Notice, each of these is *active*. As we work through the rest of this book, we'll be developing ways to implement each of these important action areas. The components also work together. For example, while I *pray* for my child each day and have personal devotions with the Lord to make sure my own attitude and focus are in line with His will, I am also *modeling* this activity in front of my child. My own action will illustrate the high priority I place on time spent with the Lord. I can also use what I have learned in my devotions to share scriptural truths with my child and to offer encouragement by discussing how the Lord has answered my prayers.

*The righteous man leads a blameless life; blessed are his children after him.*
(PROV. 20:7)

We will see the importance modeling has in every aspect of our lives. The keys to being a good model are *consistency*—our lifestyle, for as long as we live—and *servanthood*, as Jesus demonstrated. We'll discuss how to counteract the negative modeling of the world and to handle the television intrusion.

While *teaching* is not the same as training, it is a vitally important component of training. We can teach our children in many areas, including the classroom of life, wisdom and knowing God's will, and making good decisions. A necessary prerequisite to all learning is the skill of reading, and I'll offer some tips on how you can help your child become an accomplished reader.

As we teach our children, we also need to *encourage* them to use their knowledge and skills for God's glory. We must impart courage and teach them how to handle failure, while helping them to realize their unique role in the Lord's plan.

Finally, all of these elements require *discipline*. But I would like to approach discipline in a somewhat unique manner—looking beyond punishment to focus on discipleship. There are hundreds of books on the market that deal totally with discipline from a punishment aspect, and theories abound on whether spanking or "time out" is the best method. For now I'll leave that area up to you to explore on your own and settle in your heart with the Lord.

The Bible places great importance on discipline and discipleship. Discipleship is much like training, involving modeling, teaching, and encouragement. Discipleship builds *inner discipline*, and that will be our emphasis. Inner discipline is an auto-pilot reaction; it's what makes us obey the Lord when we are faced with temptation. We'll discuss how to disciple children to obey the Lord and their parents. We'll explore the cultivation of responsibility and self-management. And I'll offer some practical tips on time management, study skills, and goal attainment.

With instruction in these five key areas of training and your own Bible, you'll be well-equipped to train up your child in the way he or she should go.

What does the Bible tell us to train in?

> . . . rather, train yourself to be godly. For physical training is of some value, but godliness has value for all things, holding promise for both the present life and the life to come.
>
> (1 TIM. 4:7-8)

We must train our children, first and foremost, to be *godly*. We'll look at some other important areas of life where training also proves valuable in helping your child to succeed, such as in school, a career, and the daily necessities of life (many of which—like reading—are also vitally important for learning how to be godly). However, our main priority is to develop holiness.

While this book will be helpful in offering practical ways to apply these scriptural principles, please remember that your Bible is your best resource. The Bible says:

> All Scripture is God-breathed and is useful for teaching, rebuking, correcting and training in righteousness, so that the man of God may be thoroughly equipped for every good work.
>
> (2 TIM. 3:16-17)

Wow! Every verse of Scripture comes from God and will help you to do the very things we've just discussed: *teach, discipline, and train your child!* With his Bible, every man (or woman) of God is *"thoroughly equipped"* for life! In your Bible you have the greatest book ever written on parenting and how to be successful—principles that are just as true today as they were 2,000 years ago. *Let's use it!*

Look at how Jesus *trained* His disciples. They were His "children," and He trained them much like we should train our own children—by teaching, modeling, encouraging, praying, and disciplining. The four Gospels are a great training ground for us as we determine how best to train our children to be Christlike. How we need to use this precious resource the Lord has given us!

> *"'A student is not above his teacher. . . . It is enough for the student to be like his teacher. . . ."*
> (MATT. 10:24)

We'll never *be* God, but we should train in godliness to become more Christlike—to come as close as our human limitations allow us to being like Christ, for He is the standard of perfection and success!

## WHEN DO I START?

Whether you realize it or not, you've already started. For good or bad, you've been training your child as long as you've been his (or her) parent. He's been watching and modeling your every move, listening to your words, observing how you handle problems, and picking up on your priorities.

And training never really ends, even when our children leave home, for our children continue to observe how we live our lives, how we handle traumatic situations like the death of a spouse, cancer, or the house burning down, and so on. They will notice whether or not we turn to the Lord in those times; they will take note of our attitude and obedience. And most likely they will later follow our model when as adults they encounter similar challenges. They will even model our *parenting* as they parent their own children.

*Now* is the time to start *consciously* training your child in the way of the Lord. It's never too early to begin—and never too late to make an effort.

Training begins at day one, the day the baby is born. Actually, prayer begins even earlier; you can pray for your child even before he or she is conceived! Training a child is never simple, but it's easier if you begin as an infant. Developing good habits, attitudes, and obedience *from the start* is less difficult than trying to *re-train* an adolescent in whom undesirable traits have already taken root. But it's still worth the effort even if a great deal of re-training must occur; it's just a greater challenge, requiring more patience!

> *"Who is it he is trying to teach? To whom is he explaining his message? To children weaned from their milk, to those just taken from the breast?*

> *For it is: Do and do, do and do, rule on rule, rule on rule, a little here,*
> *a little there."*

(ISA. 28:9-10)

While training is always a constant, lifelong process, older children can comprehend teaching and reasoning better than younger children. The younger a child is, the more gradual the process of training will be.

A teacher once explained to me how she teaches kindergartners, well-known for their short attention span. She told me to imagine a board with about eight nails barely started into it. Each nail represents one thing she is trying to teach the child (or perhaps, in your case, a character trait you are training the child to have). Each day she taps each nail just a little bit, teaching the child just a little more in each area. Finally, by the end of the year, all the nails are completely flush with the board. It's been a long process, but the goal has been accomplished one small tap at a time!

So it is with training our children. While older children may be able to take stronger taps in a sitting, pounding in each nail will still be a lengthy process. Training takes place over time—working a little on faith here, a little on obedience there, and a little on self-management over there. We live in a disposable society where we expect quick results and immediate action. Training doesn't happen that way; it requires patience, perseverance, and commitment. But it really works, and it's always well worth the effort! *Training* will make your family successful!

## QUALITY VS. QUANTITY TIME

Since training takes place bit by bit, *time* is vitally important. But what kind of time?

As mentioned earlier, a study of 2,400 fifth-graders revealed that the thing they found most upsetting was that *they didn't get to spend enough time with their parents.*

Because we live in a world where both parents often need to work to support the family, many popular psychologists have assured parents that the *quantity* of time they spend with their children isn't important, only the *quality* of the time they have.

Certainly there are unavoidable circumstances that make it impossible for parents to spend the quantity of time they would like to with their family. And in such cases it's essential that the primary caregiver be someone the parents respect and would like to see their children model (because that *will* happen)—someone who will emulate the parents' values and train the children in the same way that the parents would themselves. Usually a Christian grandparent or other relative is ideal, if available. A Christian day-care center is also an option. But there is really no replacement for spending a good amount of time with your own children—as much as you possibly can—and making much of it quality time as well.

Remember, the key to having godly children is *training*. And a major element of training is *modeling*. Modeling is a lifestyle process, not something that can be squeezed into fifteen quality minutes a day. Our children need to see us in a wide variety of situations and environments.

If you don't have as much time with your children as you'd like, certainly the quality issue becomes your focus. But for those parents who are at home with their children most of the time, we must remember that *quantity* isn't enough either! Training our children involves modeling, teaching, and discipline—all quality experiences.

So what *is* quality time? Time focused on the child, time actively engaged in interaction and sharing. Some of the best quality moments are spent reading with your child, conversing (especially listening), asking your child about his or her life, and answering her questions about life in general.

Although kids' never-ending questions can at times be irritating, inquiry is a child's primary way of learning about life. These questions are a great opportunity for training! Wouldn't *you* rather answer the questions, from a godly value base, than have your child seek answers from television, friends, or a non-Christian teacher?

These three tools—*conversation*, *questions*, and *reading*—are vitally important for a child's learning academically, socially, and spiritually. The time we spend talking to them, asking and answering questions, and reading to them can be the most valuable time we spend as parents. The quality of my child's learning at home and his or her success at learning in school depend heavily on my attitude as a parent.

## WHAT ABOUT ALLOWING MY CHILD FREEDOM?

As I write this, I can just hear some readers asking, "But what about my child's freedom? Isn't such proactive training going to stifle my child's individuality? Isn't training just another word for indoctrination?"

Certainly many of today's pop psychologists would respond in this manner. First of all, let us remember that this is not *my advice*, it is *God's command!* Throughout the Bible, responsibility for a child's moral development is placed squarely on the shoulders of the parents. We are commanded to train our children in the way of the Lord.

Second, let us consider what the alternative would be. If I don't "indoctrinate" my own child, someone else will. *All children are trained by someone (for example, a teacher) or something (for example, television) in some way!* And that training is likely to be in the way of the world rather than the way of the Lord—a chance we simply can't take, since the Lord places the responsibility on us.

I love the story about Samuel Taylor Coleridge, a great English poet of the Romantic period, because it so clearly illustrates the ridiculous nature of modern-day "infringement" arguments:

> One day Samuel Coleridge was talking with a man who told him that he did not believe in giving children any religious instruction whatsoever. His theory was that the child's mind should not be prejudiced in any way. At a later age, the child would be free to choose his own religious opinions.
>
> Coleridge said nothing, but after a while he asked his visitor if he would like to see his garden. Only weeds were growing in the garden. The man looked at Coleridge in surprise and said, "Why, this is not a garden! There are nothing but weeds here!" Coleridge answered, "Well, you see, I did not want to infringe on the liberty of the garden in any way. I was just giving the garden a chance to express itself and choose its own production."

This story clearly illustrates the fallacies of today's philosophy. Certainly freedom of choice plays an important part in a child's development. But it must be guided within limitations and standards set by the parents. Children are not just miniature adults; their reasoning and decision-making skills are not as developed as an adult's. Children need, and want, guidance. Survey after survey has shown that children want their parents *to be parents*, not just their friends; they want direction and discipline.

## DEVELOPING WELL-ROUNDED CHILDREN

Parental guidance is vital in spiritual development, but is also important in many other areas. The emphasis or de-emphasis we place on activities and interests will shape our children's growth. We can give our children advantages by expanding their horizons, or we can do them a disservice by limiting their growth.

We hear much talk about the importance of being "well-rounded." But what does that really mean, and how can we raise our children to have balanced interests?

A well-rounded individual has some basic knowledge in a wide variety of interests and lives a well-balanced life. Such exposure creates a feeling of comfort in further exploration of those areas.

For instance, I was raised in a family where travel was an important and common part of our lives. I feel very comfortable in exploring new places, and when I was eighteen I went on a seven-week tour of Europe with a group of students, enjoying it very much. In traveling with my parents, we often stopped at museums and cultural and historical exhibits. Some of the students I traveled with on that tour did not have such prior experiences; so they missed out on a tremendous learning and aesthetic opportunity, preferring to spend their time shopping or in leisure activities. Since these friends had never experienced museums, they felt out of their comfort zone and missed a great chance for extra enrichment.

On the other hand, I was not raised attending rock concerts. Because I didn't have this experience, I never bought tickets when a hot new group came to town, like many of my peers did, even though I lived a mile down the street from the Pacific Amphitheater. I just never felt comfortable in that environment. I wasn't sure how to dress or behave; and quite frankly, the atmosphere frightened and intimidated me. It does to this day; so I probably will not take my children to rock concerts either. I've been to a couple of Christian pop music concerts with my husband, and those are very different; but when they are held in a large auditorium, I still feel out of my comfort zone. I'd much prefer the symphony or to hear a performer in a smaller auditorium (like at church).

Individuals who are not well-rounded may become obsessed with one or two areas of life. We've all known at least one workaholic who is so focused on business achievement that he (or she) completely neglects his family, his friends, and his personal responsibilities. His imbalance may eventually cause him to lose his wife and family. And what if he lost his job for some reason? Devastation would result because he had placed all his eggs in one basket and the basket fell.

As parents, we want to protect our children from such potential destruction. As our children grow up, we can help them cultivate a variety of interests. This will help them keep their life and any one activity or trauma in eternal perspective.

We can help our children to be successful in all areas of their life, insuring this by teaching them how to carefully plan their future.

It is wise to plan for the future, since you'll spend the rest of your life there! Proverbs 24:3-4, TLB says:

> *Any enterprise is built by wise planning, becomes strong through common sense, and profits wonderfully by keeping abreast of the facts.*

Success happens by design and commitment, not by accident. Goals can only be achieved if goals are set. You can help your children learn and plan so their lives will be filled with happiness and quality experiences. What a rich gift to give them!

Setting life goals in alignment with God's plan is important. When people just drift though their existence, trouble inevitably finds them! Satan loves to slip into a void we've left open by a lack of knowledge and direction.

At the end of this book we will look closely at how you can help your child set and attain goals. Each child will want to set his or her own personal goals in each area of life. But for now it would be helpful to set some family goals. If we are going to begin training, we need some specific areas in which to train. I've often heard it said, "If you don't have a destination in mind, you'll never get there." So let's choose some specific destinations—precise areas in which we'd like our family to succeed.

Success is our ultimate goal—becoming holy and obedient to the Lord. But in practical terms, how do we embark on this journey? There are ten major areas of life in which parents are responsible to help their family develop:

- Spiritual and church.
- Ethics, morals, character qualities and traits.
- Home and family (values and closeness).
- Social and citizenship (giving to others; responsibility).
- Self-education (learning; knowing how to learn).
- School and academic success.
- Financial stewardship and planning.
- Avocations (hobbies and interests outside of work).

- Physical fitness, health, and recreation.
- Vocation (career).

Whether a child goes to public, private, or home school, ultimately the well-rounded development of the child is the parents' responsibility and a privilege God has given to those parents in order to shape the life of one of His precious children.

You may be thinking, "These areas are so broad! Where do I begin?" Here are a few suggestions to get you started.

- Don't try to set goals in all ten areas initially.
- Perhaps you'll set goals in only one area each month. This shouldn't be a source of stress. Set a few goals that can be accomplished over the next twelve months. For example, in the area of "home and family," you may wish to set a goal of holding a weekly Family Night for the next twelve months.
- Keep your goals simple, so you can remember them easily; post them in a prominent spot as a reminder.
- Set down action steps ("baby-step" objectives to reach the larger goal).
- Keep the goals fun, so your child will learn to enjoy learning (which helps accomplish the goal of self-education mentioned above).
- Base your goals on scriptural guidelines given for these areas (use a concordance to explore a topic in the Bible).

Here are some ideas to stimulate your thinking about what kind of goals to set in the area of "spiritual and church" (place a check mark next to the ones you want to work on right away):

_____ Attend church together regularly.

_____ Get involved in church social and missions activities.

_____ Hold family Bible studies on the fundamentals of faith and becoming Christlike (building character).

_____ Begin daily devotions (maybe even just after breakfast).

_____ Pray together daily.

_____ Offer praise and thanksgiving.

_____ Select and read books on topics of interest to share with each other.

_____ Share selected Bible readings and studies on a regular basis (even at meals, perhaps with Scripture cards).

One effective way of helping your child develop an interest is to model the habits or traits you'd like to see him develop. You may wish to choose three top goals to commit yourself to model—which will greatly bless *you* as well! You can also choose three goals to teach and encourage your family. After the goals are chosen, you can develop specific action steps to help you accomplish these goals over the next twelve months.

You can also work on a goal such as "self-education" simply by providing opportunities (like books or activities) to help your family expand their horizons. Unless you tell them, they probably won't even realize what you're doing. But it might be more fun to choose new experiences together.

For example, you might set a goal of trying one new experience a month. Perhaps you've never all gone roller-skating together, attended a play, or gone fishing. Or if your family would like to develop a new skill or hobby, there are many instructive videos available to rent from your local rental store or library. Maybe you're planning to paint the house. Why not rent an instructional video so everyone, even the children, can take part? Or learn how to build something and then do it together. Or cook a gourmet meal together. All these are good ideas to get you started.

Food is another great area in which to expand your family's horizons and expose them to other cultures. When my husband and I got married, a friend gave us a gift certificate to a local Moroccan restaurant. We probably never would have tried this cuisine on our own, but we found it to be such an unusual and wonderful experience that we've been back to the restaurant many times. Try a new restaurant, or try cooking a different culture's food at home. We tried cooking Moroccan food at home, once we knew what the names of the dishes meant, and it was a lot of fun! You can even study up on the culture a little to give a presentation to your family.

There are so many wonderful experiences to try and so many things to learn. I believe it benefits all of us, not just our children, to step out and try something new. You may find a new experience you really love. Or a new way to serve the Lord! It certainly adds spice to life. I know it energizes me to step out of the mundane and do something different.

Remember, you have many years over which to help your children develop a well-rounded personality; so don't worry about doing it all *now*. But also remember that they grow up very fast, and the most effective modeling and teaching takes place at the youngest age possible. There's no time like the present to get started! But also remember, it is *never* too late to begin.

## Bringing It Home

*Applying God's Principles: Please refer to Chapter 2 for ideas on Family Night format and activities.*

**Opening:** How would you define *goals*, and why is it important to set and work toward goals?

**Scripture:** Proverbs 24:3-4.

**Discussion:** What does *enterprise* mean? (A dictionary can help.) Our family is our most important enterprise. How can we insure success for our family by wise planning? Evaluate your family's current position, and discuss directions in which the family should move and grow.

**Application:** Choose one or two areas from the "Ten Life Areas" listed in this chapter. As a family, decide upon a goal in this area or these areas. Be sure to set a time limit (preferably less than a year). It's very helpful to look up verses dealing with your goal area for guidance (use a concordance). Remember: to succeed, a goal must be in line with God's will!

1. After agreeing upon a family goal, write it down and post it where everyone can be reminded of it.

2. List several "baby steps" to take in reaching the goal, and decide which action to take first.

3. What can each person do this week to work toward the family goal? Be sure to follow up during Family Night next week to see what progress has been made and to determine the next action step. Discuss it together!

# CHAPTER 9

◆

# *The Importance of Prayer*

The Scriptures clearly illustrate the importance of prayer in every situation, and training our children is no exception. In fact, two kinds of prayer are vitally important to insure success in our efforts to train our children in the way of the Lord:

• Prayer for each child.
• Modeling prayer and devotions before them.

## PRAYING FOR YOUR CHILD

I am a firm believer in prayer. I know it works; I've seen the results with my own eyes, countless times. We worship a truly awesome and miraculous God who desires to be in fellowship with us.

Just as it would be impossible to carry on a relationship with your best friend if you never talked and listened to him or her, it is impossible for us to have a relationship with the Lord without the vital element of prayer, our means of communication with God. I can assure you, He really listens, and He really cares! He says so.

Without qualification, *the most important thing you can do for your child is to pray for him or her*. We should remember that children are not really ours. They belong to the Lord. The *care and training* of His precious children have been entrusted to us, their parents—an incredible responsibility! But they are *His* children, and

He is always watching over them. In fact, Jesus says each one has a guardian angel! We can take comfort in that.

> *"Beware that you don't look down upon a single one of these little children. For I tell you that in heaven their angels have constant access to my Father."*
>
> (MATT. 18:10, TLB)

Because of this, I believe we must give our children back to the Lord and place them in His hands through prayer. He is so much more capable than we are! I find great comfort in knowing He is in control.

You can begin praying for your child even before he or she is born—even before he or she is conceived! As I write this book, I am pregnant. My husband and I have been praying for our children, in general, since we planned on marrying. In fact, I've been praying for my future children since before I even knew my husband! And we've been specifically praying for this child since the moment we discovered I was carrying him (we're having a boy).

What do we pray for? Well, the obvious, of course—that the baby will be healthy. But we pray for so much more than that. We've already dedicated this child to the Lord in our hearts and have placed his care in the hands of God. We pray that this child will learn to love and obey the Lord and follow Christ's model. We pray that we will have the wisdom and energy to train this child in the ways of the Lord, as is His will. We even pray for another baby that may or may not yet be born—the one our child will someday marry. We pray that the parents of that other child will follow the Lord and train our baby's future spouse to love and fear God.

Have you heard the song by Wayne Watson, "Somewhere in the World"? In it, he prays for a little girl who is growing up "out there somewhere," because someday his son will need a godly wife. It makes me cry to hear it, and even now just to think about it. The song is so precious because this is such a vitally important prayer that we should all be praying for our children!

I know God hears this prayer, for I know my parents prayed for me, and for my husband, since before I was even born. And miraculously enough, I am now married to an incredibly godly man, and my parents couldn't be more pleased with God's answer. I dated a number of unsuitable beaux and even seriously considered marrying someone who was totally wrong and was not walking closely with the

Lord. But my parents' prayers were answered because they never gave up!

Interestingly, I didn't even know about this until after I'd chosen Tim to be my partner for life. He is truly a gift from God, and I thank my godly parents for their unceasing prayer. The Bible so aptly says:

*The effectual fervent prayer of a righteous man availeth much.*

(JAS. 5:16, KJV)

I'm sure there were times when my parents felt frustrated with many of the bad choices I made in my life. They probably despaired that I would ever "turn out." But God is faithful, and He promises that if we train up our children in His ways, they will not depart from it. Unfortunately, sometimes a child is living within the confines of the consequences of his or her ungodly choices (a bad marriage, etc.) by the time they come back to the Lord. I encourage you to stick it out; never give up on your kids, and never think it's too late. Just keep praying!

God always answers a righteous parent's prayers on behalf of his or her child. Look at how God responded to Abraham:

*And Abraham said to God, "If only Ishmael might live under your blessing!" Then God said . . . "And as for Ishmael, I have heard you: I will surely bless him; I will make him fruitful and will greatly increase his numbers."*

(GEN. 17:18-20)

God answered Abraham's prayers for Ishmael.

Job, one of the most righteous men ever to walk this earth, provides us with a wonderful model of his daily custom of praying for, and on behalf of, his children, in Job 1:5:

*Early in the morning he would sacrifice a burnt offering for each of them, thinking, "Perhaps my children have sinned and cursed God in their hearts." This was Job's regular custom.*

Consistent, fervent, unfailing prayer *is* effective. In Luke 18:1-8 Jesus offers His disciples a parable to show the importance of always praying and never giving up. He tells of a judge, who was not a godly or caring man, and a widow who constantly pled with the judge to grant her justice against her adversary. Finally, after some time and perseverance by the widow, the judge gave in, just because he was sick of having her bother him constantly. Then Jesus said:

> "Listen to what the unjust judge says. And will not God bring about justice for his chosen ones, who cry out to him day and night? Will he keep putting them off? I tell you, he will see that they get justice, and quickly. However, when the Son of Man comes, will he find faith on earth?"
>
> (LUKE 18:6-8)

To protect our children and insure their success, we must pray for our children unceasingly and have faith that the Lord will answer. I might suggest, also, that you pray *with* your spouse. Not only is this spiritual closeness a great blessing to your marriage, but the Bible says your prayers will be answered:

> "Again, I tell you that if two of you on earth agree about anything you ask for, it will be done for you by my Father in heaven."
>
> (MATT. 18:19)

## MODELING PRAYER AND DEVOTIONS

Just as it is important to pray for your children, it is important for your children to see you pray. By praying and holding your own personal devotions in front of your children, they will see the importance you place on spending special time alone with the Lord. You will be modeling this important behavior that you would like to see your child develop.

I've had many great models in this area, and I'd like to share a few with you to illustrate the impact they had on my life. Over the years I often saw my parents pray, but I especially remember my dad's habit, to this day, of reading his Bible before going to bed each night. He didn't make a big thing of it; in fact, he never said a word. He just did it. I believe that had a great impact on my own practice of reading each night before going to sleep, and first thing in the morning as well.

My dad reads his Bible through an average of two and a half times a year. This knowledge has made me realize the Bible isn't daunting because of its size. If I plug along, a little each day, I will get through it (and I will again feel that wonderful sense of accomplishment).

My Aunt Donna is one of the most godly women I know. She

always has been, since I was a little girl. Even though she's always lived about eight hours away from my home, she's had a tremendous impact on my spiritual life through modeling prayer and devotion. Whenever I visited my Aunt Donna, or when we'd all get together at the family cabin for holidays, I always observed her spending quiet time alone, reading her Bible, writing in her prayer notebook, and praying. She wouldn't hide away either; she'd do it mid-morning, in her bedroom with the door open, or at the table.

As a young child I was always curious. I'd kind of hang around to see what she was doing; and I always admired her, so I wanted to be included. She'd never let us kids interrupt her, but she'd quietly explain this was her quiet time with the Lord and she'd include us, often making me want to go have my own quiet time.

First Thessalonians 5:16-18 tells us what behavior we are to model. My Aunt Donna is the perfect example of this passage:

*Be joyful always; pray continually; give thanks in all circumstances, for this is God's will for you in Christ Jesus.*

You know, my Aunt Donna has gone through more trials and tribulations than most people I've ever heard of. She has also been greatly blessed by the Lord. Through it all I've never seen her faith falter, or her joy. She now has a rare neurological disorder that is somewhat like multiple sclerosis. She is losing her ability to walk and control involuntary spasms. Yet she runs several home decoration shops and is a wonderful mother and always a servant of her Lord.

Through all the difficulties, she is joyful, humorous, and thankful. I am grateful for her godly model of prayer and devotion.

Earlier in the book I wrote of my friend who has watched her family's prayers being answered time after time as they adopted more children. What a great model we can be to our children as they see our family's prayers answered!

When I try to remember the times I felt closest to my family growing up, I think of times we spent praying together. It's great for our kids to see us in private prayer and devotion, and also very special for them to share in those moments. Family Night offers a great opportunity for prayer together, as do mealtimes. We can praise the Lord together as a family in good times and bad and can rely on Him through prayer to get us through difficulties.

## HANDLING TRAGEDY TOGETHER

One of the most difficult events ever to occur in my family was when my brother, Cary, and his wife, Alexa, lost their twin boys at birth. One was stillborn, full-term, because of toxemia Alexa had contracted a week earlier. The other was born with the umbilical cord around his neck and could not be resuscitated. Talk about a tragedy! We'd all so looked forward to this wonderful event, and the news was shocking! Then, as if the loss of the twins was not enough, Alexa almost died of childbirth fever.

I'll never forget the day Cary called from the delivery room to tell us the news. Our little family was gathered together at a summer cabin in Lake Tahoe, two hours from Cary's house. We were awaiting his call, to hear of the joyous birth. My dad answered the phone with anticipation, but we knew something was wrong when his face quickly fell. "Oh, Cary, I'm so sorry. We'll pray for Alexa right now, and then we'll be right down."

We all waited with dread as he hung up the phone, tears rolling down his face. He didn't even have to say anything. The four of us (my sister wasn't born yet) all ran into a bedroom, threw ourselves on the bed, and wept uncontrollably. My parents didn't try to act tough. They shared this sorrow with us. They modeled a real response of grief.

We cried for awhile. Then we sat on the bed together, held hands, and prayed for a long time. My parents gave the whole situation to the Lord. They let go of their lost grandsons, knowing they were in God's hands. We all prayed desperately for Alexa, who lay in the hospital fighting for her life, and for Cary, who was quickly losing everyone he loved.

I can't tell you what a difficult time this was for our family. It is so hard for me to write this, to see the computer through my tears, even now, sixteen years later.

After turning to the Lord with our pain and receiving His strength and courage, we piled into the car and rushed down the mountain. We prayed for Alexa and Cary as we went and took comfort in knowing the Lord was in control and all was for the best. Because of His grace, God answered our prayers and miraculously healed Alexa. Years later God blessed Cary and Alexa with two beautiful girls (not twins).

This event really shaped my life. Perhaps you can think of such a tragedy in your own childhood. Or maybe you've already shared one with your own children. How we handle these difficult times in our lives is so important; it really shows who we are.

Personally, I saw my parents practice what they preach. They showed real emotions, and they modeled the right way to handle a tragedy. No one ever blamed God. We gave it all to Him and took comfort in his power and love. We turned to the Lord in prayer *first*— that was our automatic response! Since that moment, it has almost always been my auto-pilot response in times of trouble, so powerful an impact did this training, through unconscious modeling, have on my life.

## Bringing It Home

*Applying God's Principles: Please refer to Chapter 2 for ideas on Family Night format and activities.*

**Opening:** Why is prayer important? What kinds of things can we pray to God about?

**Scripture:** Acts 4:23-31.

**Discussion:** Discuss what that prayer meant, pointing out the main components: recognizing God's power and sovereignty; acknowledging the Lord's control of their situation and that His will would be done; asking that He be glorified; the answer to the prayer.

**Application:**
1. Does God always answer prayer? (Yes. He may answer, "yes," "no," or "later.")
2. Read 1 John 3:22. Why do we receive what we ask for? What kind of motive should we have?
3. As a family, recall times in the past when God has answered your prayers.
4. Each person can put forth one prayer request; then trade amongst the family so that each person prays for one other person's request throughout the upcoming week. At your next Family Night, discuss whether prayers have been answered yet.
5. This would be a good time to begin a family prayer notebook in which you can keep track of answers to prayer.

# CHAPTER 10

◆

# *How to Be a Good Model*

Children imitate their parents. We've all seen the phenomenon of little girls at age four or five who suddenly "must wear make-up and high heels" so they can "be like Mommy." Or the seven-year-old son who takes apart the vacuum cleaner so he can "fix it like Daddy does." Imitating Mommy and Daddy is an important part of a child's development. Such modeling enables a little girl to learn to be a woman, to see what a wife does, to know how to mother and care for a home. Little boys, modeling their fathers, learn how to treat women, how to "act like a man," how to use their strength, and what it means to be a dad.

Modeling may be more obvious in young children, as they play-act parental behaviors or (to a mother's astonishment) actually want to help with and learn how to perform household chores! But the process continues throughout the term of the parent-child relationship. Teen-age boys will likely treat their girlfriends with the same respect and manners (or lack thereof) that they observe in their father's treatment of their mother. A teen-age girl can model her mother's demure gentleness, or her promiscuous flirtations. Eventually our children will develop a marriage relationship based in part on observations of *our* marriages; they will even form opinions on what an elderly lifestyle is like based on what they see in their own parents.

It is impossible to overemphasize the importance of modeling. The

Scriptures clearly emphasize the impact of modeling and instruct us in *how* to be good models.

## WHAT KIND OF MODEL SHOULD I BE?

There are really two kinds of models: those who exemplify a godly lifestyle and those who do not. We see the impact of *negative* parental models in these Scriptures:

> He [Ahaziah] did evil in the eyes of the Lord, because he walked in the ways of his father and mother and in the ways of Jeroboam son of Nebat, who caused Israel to sin.
>
> (1 KINGS 22:52)

> "Instead, they have followed the stubbornness of their hearts; they have followed the Baals, as their fathers taught them."
>
> (JER. 9:14)

> He [Ahaziah] too walked in the ways of the house of Ahab, for his mother encouraged him in doing wrong.
>
> (2 CHRON. 22:3)

These three examples point to children who went bad, and God lays the blame squarely at the feet of the parents who failed to model holiness and a righteous lifestyle pleasing to the Lord. We've all seen tragic modern-day examples of bad parental models as well—broken marriages, child abuse, alcohol and drug abuse, irresponsible behavior, atheism. We've seen young children who use bad language and bully other children because they're modeling the behavior seen in their parents.

The tragedy of child abuse, passed down from generation to generation, perfectly illustrates the damage negative parental modeling can cause. Even when the adult child realizes how terrible abuse is and determines not to repeat the abuse, he (or she) often finds himself abusing his own children in the way he himself suffered. How is this explained? *Training* puts you on auto-pilot. Your initial reactions or actions will be in accordance with the way you were trained, the primary models you observed. This training is hard to break, good or bad. Christian parents want their children to receive positive, godly training, so they will be on auto-pilot when tempted by sin. I think most of us would like to be the kind of godly model that the Bible praises. Future generations are truly affected by the sins or righteousness of their parents and grandparents, through the process of modeling. As Paul says of Timothy:

> *I have been reminded of your sincere faith, which first lived in your grandmother Lois and in your mother Eunice and, I am persuaded, now lives in you also.*
>
> (2 TIM. 1:5)

Let this be an encouragement to grandparents as well! Perhaps you are disappointed in the model your own children are providing for your grandchildren. Please know that you can have a tremendous impact by your own godly model. And if your children are doing a great job, you can reinforce their model with your own.

## EXACTLY *HOW* CAN I BE A GOOD MODEL?

We want to be good parents and good models to our children, but sometimes it is hard to know how to do this in *practical terms*. The Bible offers us a wealth of guidance, instructing us in exactly what we should model and how to do it. There are *five major areas of importance*. As parents, we should model to our children:

- A consistent Christian lifestyle.
- Servanthood.
- Integrity.
- Success.
- A godly marriage.

We are not only models; we are ourselves following other models. If I had to decide what to model and do it on my own, I would be in big trouble. Fortunately I have the perfect model to follow—Christ. Perhaps your parents weren't great models—maybe they weren't even Christians; but you now desire to be a godly model to your children. You don't need the model of your own parents anymore. As Christians, the model provided by our Heavenly Father takes precedence over any earthly model we could look to (whether our parents were good examples or not), since He and Jesus alone are perfect.

> *Be imitators of God, therefore, as dearly loved children and live a life of love, just as Christ loved us and gave himself up for us as a fragrant offering and sacrifice to God.*
>
> (EPH. 5:1-2)

We are to imitate and model God. Through Christ we are provided with a human-divine model, one of perfect holiness. If we follow this verse and "live a life of love" as Christ did, dedicating our lives to the Lord as living sacrifices, then we will be great models to our children. The closer our lives conform to Christ's example, the better models we will be—automatically!

Of course, no matter how hard we try, we will always fall short of the glory of Christ. We are sinful human beings, and we are bound to make mistakes. One of the great benefits of modeling Christ in your own life is that your children will see *who you model* and they will follow your example; they too will learn to imitate Christ foremost. Following Christ above all others can be encouraged through instruction as well as modeling.

## A CONSISTENT CHRISTIAN LIFESTYLE

Your *daily lifestyle*, the way you interact with other people and your family and how you handle ups and downs, all reflect your relationship with the Lord. Our children develop attitudes by watching the way we do things. They form the very habits and attitudes that they observe us modeling. Our children will know (or conclude), by the consistency of our actions and attitudes, whether we are truly modeling Christ—trying hard to walk in holiness—or whether we are hypocrites. They will then follow suit. It is almost inevitable.

The Bible offers examples of the type of lifestyle we should be modeling to our children:

> *And we pray this in order that you may live a life worthy of the Lord and may please him in every way: bearing fruit in every good work, growing in the knowledge of God.*
> (COL. 1:10)

> *Whoever claims to live in him must walk as Jesus did.*
> (1 JOHN 2:6)

> *You already know how to please God in your daily living, for you know the commands we gave you from the Lord Jesus himself. Now we beg you—yes, we demand of you in the name of the Lord Jesus—that you live more and more closely to that ideal.*
> (1 THESS. 4:1-2, TLB)

We are to follow Christ's model. To do this, we need to learn about His life, observe His actions, and obey His instructions. Being a good model for our children *requires us to be in the Word*, studying Jesus' example in the New Testament, and to be in constant prayer and worship, seeking the Lord's will for our lives. Remember, our children do as we *do*, not as we *say*—always!

Living the Christian lifestyle to which God has called us, in obedience to Him and seeking His will, will make us successful. We must remember this: true success is the goal we have set for training; and to help our children achieve that goal, we ourselves must be striving toward it also.

In modeling, we add another important element to insure success: *consistency.* Our successful lifestyle must be consistent if it is to impact our children. Kids can tell when we're sincere and committed, or if we're just "going through a phase." To raise a successful family, you can't just take the biblical knowledge from this book and get on a two-month "kick" of training, then go back to your old lifestyle. It's a lifetime commitment.

For training to be successful, it must be consistent. *Modeling is not a project—it's a lifestyle.*

Sure, I make many mistakes, and you will too. We are all human. There are times when we show a wrong attitude or we fail to obey the Lord as we should. Or we get caught up in our own pursuits and put our relationship with God on the back burner. But did you know that these situations can be turned around and their negative impact lessened, and that we can use these times to model self-correction to our child?

Later in this book we will look at self-management, but here's a little preview of how to teach this important tool to your child. Let's say you are having a really bad day. It's over 100 degrees outside, and the air conditioner isn't working; the dog jumped the fence, and you can't find him; your spouse is home sick with the flu; and little Laura whines, "I'm hot, and I want an ice cream!" for the twentieth time. You finally snap, "Join the crowd! I'm hot, too, and I'm sick and tired of listening to you whine. Just go to your room and shut up!"

Minutes later, when you've calmed down, you feel bad about snapping. Of course a four-year-old would be complaining and miserable; so are you, and you're an adult! Laura did need to stop whining, but you wish you'd handled it differently. Now what can you do?

When situations like this occur, or something even worse, you can help to correct your actions by sitting down with your child and modeling the right response to your wrong behavior. For example, you could say: "Sweetheart, I'm so sorry I snapped at you. What you were doing was wrong, but I should have corrected you by sending you to your room, not by saying the things I did. I love you. Jesus would not like my attitude, would He? I should have reacted with patience and kindness. Will you forgive me, please? I will try to do better next time. We both will. Will you pray with me to ask God's forgiveness and ask Him to help me have a better attitude?" (It is now likely that the child will want to pray about her own attitude as well, and you can encourage that.)

Admitting I'm wrong doesn't come easy to me. You may find it difficult as well. But our children respect us when we are honest with them, and they will respect our consistent action of realizing our easy disobedience to the Lord, seeking forgiveness, and trying to do better. *Being vulnerable before our children teaches them powerful lessons.*

How might this model rub off on your child? Perhaps in a few days he or she will treat a playmate poorly. Then when the friend gets hurt feelings, your child may realize her poor behavior and feel sad about it. Since she saw how you handled such a situation, she too will feel the need to apologize, then seek the Lord's forgiveness and try to do better next time.

This valuable lesson is rarely modeled and therefore is so very difficult for most children to develop as a habit.

Let us clarify, however, the difference between parental actions that the Lord would not approve of (when an apology is appropriate) and purposeful actions. When a child is corrected or punished in love, not anger, in a purposeful manner, then the parent should not apologize for the action, even when it is painful.

## SERVANTHOOD

The center point of Jesus' lifestyle, and the basis of His ministry, was servanthood. He commands us to act in this manner as well. He says:

> *"But among you it is quite different. Anyone wanting to be a leader among you must be your servant. And if you want to be right at the top, you must serve like a slave. Your attitude must be like my own, for I, the Messiah, did not come to be served, but to serve, and to give my life as a ransom for many."*
> (MATT. 20:26-28, TLB)

Wow! Servanthood is a tough concept to accept. Jesus said that if we are to be great and are to be leaders, we must be servants. And the greatest among us is like a slave! How do we do this as parents?

If we are to model Christ, we must model *servanthood*, for that was His very mission on earth, as He says in this verse.

What pops into your mind when you hear the word *servant*? "But people will walk all over me. How can I be a leader—I'll have no authority?" Certainly, servanthood is not a popular concept in today's culture, often not even among Christians. But Christ puts tremendous importance upon service and servanthood.

Did Christ have the problems that we automatically anticipated? Did people walk all over Him, or did He lack authority? Certainly not. He was the greatest leader ever to walk this earth. But He never demanded His rights. He never lorded His position over His disciples or the people. He gently instructed them and served them with love and compassion.

That is how we are to serve our children—with love and compassion rather than in an authoritarian manner. My parents always loved me in such a way that I knew, without them having to say it, that they placed the needs of myself and my siblings above their own. They hardly ever bought new clothes. They often canceled plans they would've enjoyed because of an opportunity that meant a lot to us. They were very loving and giving, yet fully the leaders of the family. Servanthood is the heart of leadership.

It might help to think of servanthood in a business context. I used to be the national operations manager at Citizens for Excellence in Education before I became vice president. At that time, my duties included personnel management and coordination of all work activities. I tried to practice leadership through servanthood. I had observed my father's model in doing this for many years and found it to be very effective.

Just as my father had, I wanted to make our staff feel that I really cared about them (because I really did). I would ask about their concerns, listen, and try to resolve any difficulties. When the workload got heavy, I'd pitch in and help. Because our office worked on the servanthood principle, you'd often find all of us—president, vice president, and operations manager—working alongside part-time clerical help, madly stuffing and sealing envelopes to get an important mailing out.

When your employees realize that you truly have their best interests at heart, that you're willing to work alongside them and not feel "above" doing their job duties, that you can get yourself a cup of coffee instead of yelling for someone to serve you, then they are more likely to give you their full effort. Because they know you care, they care. They are willing to sacrifice and stay late, doing whatever it takes to make the team a success.

The same principle works within families. The parents are the leaders, but the children are not slaves. The family is a team; and when the children know the parents really care and are doing everything to help serve them, the children will be more likely to work with the parents and follow their lead. Servanthood builds confidence in the leader and a feeling of security in the team.

Sadly, many parents look at their children as being there to do the work and take care of the parents when they get old. But Jesus places great value on children.

> Then he [Jesus] said to them, "Whoever welcomes this little child in my name welcomes me; and whoever welcomes me welcomes the one who sent me. For he who is least among you all—he is the greatest."
> (LUKE 9:48)

We should value our children the way God values them. Not the way the world looks at children—as disposable "fetuses"—but as the "greatest of all," like Jesus said. In Matthew 19:14 Jesus made time in His busy schedule to simply spend time with children. So should we. To live a successful lifestyle modeled after Christ, we must *serve* our children and model to them our servanthood of others.

## INTEGRITY

How many times have you covered for your spouse, telling someone on the phone that "He/she is not home yet"? Have you ever been rude to a salesperson on the phone, rather than gently saying, "No, thank you" and hanging up? When someone from the school asked you to help with the school carnival, did you decline, saying you had to work when actually you just didn't feel like helping? These common and seemingly innocent occurrences become quite convicting when we realize the impact they have on our children. One mother told me a story of her child lying to the teacher about why her homework was late. When she asked the child what would cause her to lie, when she knows Jesus tells us to be honest, her daughter said, "Well, I heard you make up a story to that man on the phone, so I thought it's okay to make an excuse and it isn't really a lie."

Ouch! Our children are very observant!

If I am to model a successful, godly lifestyle to my child, I must be beyond reproach. I believe that to keep my integrity intact, I must watch my tongue in everything, even little, unimportant things, to insure that I am completely honest and never misleading—even avoiding the sin of omission! We all know that sometimes the truth we *don't* tell can be even worse than the lie we do tell.

The *New World Dictionary* defines integrity as "the quality or state of being of sound moral principle; uprightness, honesty and sincerity."

The Bible says:

*Righteousness guards the man of integrity, but wickedness overthrows the sinner.*
(PROV. 13:6)

*Righteousness* can be defined as knowing right from wrong and doing what is right. Righteousness requires action, a holy lifestyle, and the utmost integrity. A successful, godly lifestyle demands that we live righteously, above reproach. To help our children be successful, we must model this integrity in the big and little occurrences of daily life.

## MODELING SUCCESS

Since our ultimate goal in training our children is to see them become a success in God's eyes, to train them in His ways, we must carefully model this type of lifestyle. They will know our own view of success by the values and attitudes that direct our behavior. They don't expect us to be perfect, but they know when we try.

In providing our children a model for success, it's not only important that we *be* good models, but that we direct our children to other godly models. For example, Jesus is always the best model of godly success, while movie stars are often worldly models.

There are basically these two kinds of success: worldly and godly. An examination of the lives of people with success in these two areas reveals vastly different types of achievement and lifestyles. Compare the two lists. You may find it helpful to use these lists as a tool in explaining to your child the importance of becoming a godly success—a lifestyle achiever—and finding good and godly role models. The first list here fits some of those we view as a *worldly* success.

## Characteristics of Worldly Success

- Momentary achiever (i.e., success only in a single area of life such as sports, entertainment, or business).
- Extremely focused.
- Chaotic personal life.
- Generally self-centered.
- Needs to prove him/herself.
- Discontentment.
- Dependent on external supports (having the latest car, going to the "in" restaurant, having friends who build his ego).
- Heavily influenced or guided by trends.
- Humanistic/atheistic viewpoint.

## Characteristics of Godly Success

- Lifestyle achievers.
- Stable personal life.
- Generally others-centered (servanthood).
- Self-confident (identity in Christ is secure).
- Content but not stagnant.
- Internal strength (strength from the Lord).
- Long-term values (righteousness—knowing right from wrong and doing what's right).
- Godly viewpoint.

Imagine the people you know who are successful by God's standards. How would you describe them? Perhaps you would use words like honest, loving, positive, joyful, wise, courageous, obedient, friendly, hard-working, compassionate, patient, responsible, reliable, full of integrity, dependable.

Notice that these words are all attitudes or character qualities rather than skills. These involve the very heart of who the person is— his or her lifestyle and values—not his or her accomplishments. These characteristics can be taught and modeled by parents, and children can learn them. It's who the person *is* that makes them successful, not what they do. Because of who they are, they will naturally do what's right, what is God's will. By modeling these qualities and attitudes to your children, you can help them become successful. To get started, ask yourself the following questions:

1. *What characteristics do I need to teach my child?* Make a list (you can use those I mentioned to get started), then choose one or two qualities to begin working on. For example, you may choose "patience."
2. *How will I model this characteristic to my child?* List ways in which you can teach this quality to your child by modeling it in your own behavior. For example: begin showing her how you are patient with others and with her. Demonstrate patience by your actions.
3. *What will I encourage?* Encourage development of those traits that your child already exhibits. For example, if he already shows signs of wisdom, discuss with your son how this wisdom will benefit him in school when lessons such as evolution or sex education are taught. Help him to develop the trait by seeking God's wisdom from the Bible and applying it to his life.

## MODELING A GOOD MARRIAGE

When my husband and I got married, our pastor told us what a great advantage it was to our own marriage that both of us came from solid homes where our parents are still married to each other. Statistics show that children from broken homes are more likely to end their own marriages in divorce than are those from homes where parents stayed together.

Why is this? Because children model their parents. If they see their parents give up on marriage, they are more likely to do so when their own marriage goes through rough times. Also, children from broken homes are less likely to have seen healthy conflict resolution skills displayed between their parents; so they never learn to solve problems and to stay committed rather than running away from conflict.

Perhaps you and your spouse are already divorced. Does this mean it's too late for your children? No. But you will have to work especially hard to offer your children a good marriage role model— perhaps their grandparents, your new marriage with another spouse, or close friends of the family. Rather than ignoring the past and figuring it's only your own business, it might be helpful to talk things through with your children and explain how the problem could have or should have been resolved and to reaffirm the importance of marriage commitment. Share openly and honestly.

For those of us who do have intact marriages, we should not be complacent in thinking that simply because we are together we are being a good model of marriage. I know of some marriages where the parents are still together, but the children are seeing a model of a bad marriage, perhaps worse in some ways than if the parents were separated.

Just because we're together doesn't mean we're modeling a *good* marriage. Do we love and serve each other? Do we treat one another with respect? Do we follow the biblical mandates for marriage? Do we build one another up, or do we criticize and blame? Do we complain about our spouse to our friends or support him or her? Are we loving and affectionate? Do we meet each other's needs?

And even if we have a good marriage, we may not be *modeling* it. Do we do "our own thing" in most of life and save quality time together for the bedroom? Or do we allow our children to see how much we really love one another by holding hands, dreaming about our future, snuggling on the couch? Do your children hear you sincerely tell your spouse you love him or her? Do your actions show it? Do you build your spouse up in front of and to the children?

We must recognize that it's not enough to *have* a good marriage; we need to let our children *see* it. We'd all like to have our children end up in good, healthy, God-centered marriages, right? Well, we're training them for it right now, whether we realize it or not, by the way we conduct our own marriage in front of them. They're likely to follow the patterns we exhibit.

If you keep your love and affection private, your children may not realize it exists. My parents always showed their warmth by a quick hug and kiss at the kitchen sink or by holding hands in the car. As a child, these little gestures were reassuring to me. They did not go unobserved because they reassured me that my parents loved one another and would stay together. We shouldn't underestimate the importance of the *security* this provides for our children. When children feel secure in their family and home environment, they are set free to learn, explore, grow, and achieve.

You can also model things like family decision-making, goal planning, and budgeting—important activities of marriage—by bringing these items together to the Lord, as a family, and working through them.

## KEYS TO MODELING

To sum up the process of becoming a positive model for our children, I would like to stress that modeling is part of every moment, every facet, of our lives. Modeling is a lifelong, constant process involving our lifestyles. Consistency is vital to our success.

Lawrence O. Richards, author of *The Word Parents Handbook*, outlines seven ingredients of being an effective model:

1. Frequent, long-term contact with the model.
2. A warm, loving relationship with the model.
3. Exposure to the inner states of the model. That is, models need to share what they feel and think.
4. Opportunity to observe the model in a variety of life situations.
5. Consistency and clarity in the model's behavior and values.
6. Correspondence between the model's behavior and expressed beliefs.
7. An explanation in words of the model's lifestyle. That is, models need to tell as well as show the truths and principles that guide their actions.

This summation by Mr. Richards reiterates what we have learned through scriptural principles. To train our children, we need to:

- Spend quality and quantity time with them.
- Love and serve them.
- Be real, open, and honest with them.
- Be consistent and full of integrity in our actions.
- Teach them the principles we are modeling.

## HANDLING OUTSIDE MODELS

Training our children would be so much easier if they were exposed only to our model and to godly models in the Bible. Unfortunately, the world we live in brings them into daily contact with many other models—many of which are ungodly.

What other models influence your child?

- Television.
- Peers.
- Music lyrics.
- School teachers and curriculum.
- Advertising.

Of course, the list could go on and on, but these major influences are in the lives of virtually every child. Of this list, perhaps the greatest impact is made at school and by television (if your child has access to one).

For example, by the end of sixth grade most children will have spent approximately 6,000 hours at school. Being vice president of Citizens for Excellence in Education, I have seen the tremendous negative influence public schools can have on children. Promiscuity is encouraged in sex education classes, God is mocked in evolutionary science instruction, and children are taught to seek their own "inner god" and "spirit guides" through New-Age self-esteem programs. Public schools can have a tremendously negative spiritual influence on our children; yet 90 percent of Christian children remain in those public school classrooms.

But don't be discouraged! Did you realize that in that same length of time, your child has spent 60,000 waking hours at home with you? That means you have *ten times* the opportunity to offer a godly model! You can provide your child with solid, biblical instruction at home to counteract the worldly teaching he or she receives at school, and you can alert her to the false teaching she may receive and instruct her on how to handle it.

You can also get involved with other parents to eliminate such negative spiritual elements from the public schools and replace them with moral values. For one thing, you can contact CEE (the address and phone number are at the end of this book) for assistance. They have a successful plan to help reform your school.

So, of that 60,000 hours children are at home, what are they doing? Many of them are sitting in front of the television. A study just released in the fall of 1993 by the U.S. Department of Education found that 20 percent of fourth graders, 14 percent of eighth graders, and 6 percent of twelfth-graders reported watching *six or more hours of television per day!* That's a lot of television!

Hopefully, their parents aren't letting them watch all the sex and violence of prime-time television. Maybe they're watching children's programming. Wait—rewind. One study recently quoted in *USA Weekend* puts the number of violent episodes at five per hour in prime time and *32 per hour in Saturday-morning cartoons!* We all know how bad prime time is, but cartoons are six times as bad! It looks like most TV is providing pretty bad modeling, too. In the next chapter we'll talk more about how to handle the television.

So, how can you help to prevent this negative modeling? First of all, realize you can't eliminate it entirely—unless the Rapture comes.

We all live in a sinful world, and instead of running away from it, we need to teach our children to be strong in spite of it (while still protecting them as much as possible). Here are some tips for counteracting the negative influences surrounding your children:

- Spend as much time training your children as possible, modeling godly success, so that your proportionate influence will be greater than that of the world (in terms of quality *and* quantity).
- Help your children develop peers from Christian families, through Sunday school and church activities, especially as their close friends.
- Encourage your child to be involved in mostly Christian and church activities and clubs as much as possible; this provides more godly modeling.
- If your children attend public school, carefully examine their curricula and textbooks and counteract any ungodly teaching, at home. It certainly doesn't hurt to do this with Christian school curricula also since, unfortunately, some Christian schools use secular materials.
- Control television viewing carefully. See the next chapter for more suggestions on TV.
- Listen to your child's music, and screen out those lyrics that are clearly inappropriate. Buy them music by Christian artists in the popular styles they like, so they'll have greater access to it; and keep your own radio tuned to a Christian station.
- Have Christian videos and cartoons available as an alternative to secular television.
- When you see false advertising, or ads using sex to sell a product, explain the techniques to your children so they will be wise and not fooled by tricks of the trade.

### Bringing It Home

*Applying God's Principles: Please refer to Chapter 2 for ideas on Family Night format and activities.*

Opening:      Read the lists of characteristics of worldly success vs. godly success. Which kind of success is better? Why?

Scripture:    Zechariah 7:9-10; Philippians 2:3-4; and Colossians 3:12.

**Discussion:** Based on these passages, how does God want us to treat others? What is *compassion* (you may wish to use a dictionary)? Is compassion others-centered or self-centered? Which kind of successful person would treat others this way?

**Application:**
1. Discuss the meaning of servanthood.
2. Each person should share three ways he or she can be a servant to others. Pick one way to be a servant to others in your family this week (you may wish to choose secretly, then next week see if you can guess what each person did to serve the others).
3. Jesus was a servant to others. How did he treat people? How should we treat people?
4. Should we consider ourselves better than anyone else?
5. Each person can think of one other person, at school or at work, to whom they can show compassion.

# CHAPTER 11

◆

# *Television:*
# *The Great Intruder*

Television, the greatest outside influence to intrude upon our homes, poses a tremendous threat to our family cohesion, our children's values, and even our children's development, if we do not properly control it. A former colleague of mine once called it the "plug-in drug."

Certainly television does have its benefits as well. I know my family enjoys many of the programs carried on The Discovery Channel; we've learned a great deal about history, home repair, crafts, and more. Some children's learning shows can be beneficial, and we all find the news, some talk shows, and round-table political discussions to be informative. Even a few good family sitcoms remain to provide relaxing entertainment.

The key to making the most of our families' television viewing is careful *selection* of quality programs and *moderation* in viewing.

Unfortunately, in many homes the television is virtually always running, and children are the primary viewers and selectors of programming. The average television set is on for *seven hours each day!* Wow! Who do you think the children model in those families?

Our nation's *three-year-olds* now watch as much TV as the ten-year-olds—an average of *thirty hours each week!* This means that by the time a child enters first grade he has seen more than 5,000 hours of television. (By the time he turns seventeen, he's viewed approximately 15,000 hours of programming.)

Well, what if all 5,000 hours were quality, educational programming? Then would such viewing be appropriate? Personally I don't think so. What the child is viewing is important, but just as important is *what the child is missing*. A child watching that much television does not have time to read, play outdoors with other children, interact closely with the parents in creative learning opportunities, play make-believe games, or do art projects. The child is not developing his imaginative and social skills while watching television.

The average teen spends twenty hours each week watching television. While the quantity of viewing has decreased (due to increased time demands by school and extracurricular activities), the quality of viewing has usually deteriorated. Music videos (primarily MTV) and movie channels are their preferred choice—most of which convey objectionable worldly themes.

What message are teens receiving from such programming? Sex, violence, and drugs are popular themes in music videos and many movies. Perhaps most surprising to parents are the liberal political messages that are literally indoctrinating our youth. Sit down and watch MTV for fifteen minutes—I guarantee you'll be shocked.

Our kids are receiving "politically correct" messages about environmentalism, world religion (the New Age), abortion, and contraception. They are also being manipulated into liberal political action, as evidenced by the success of MTV's 1992 "Get out the Vote" campaign, in which viewers were subjected to biased information about the candidates and encouraged to vote for Bill Clinton.

## TV'S HIDDEN DANGERS

Television's most obvious threat is to *family values*. Which exerts the greatest influence on your child's values—quality time spent with you or time in front of the TV set?

Certainly effects on the development of children's morals and depictions of violence and sex are of the greatest concern. But television also poses a threat to your family in other important ways that aren't commonly discussed.

• Television *denigrates the value of religion* by leaving it out of the lives of TV families (or ridiculing it openly). God is rarely portrayed in a positive light, and Christianity is viewed only as "religion," not as a dynamic relationship. Children could easily come to the conclusion that their own family is "weird" for putting such an emphasis on Jesus and the church, since TV families (which represent "everyone else") don't live like your family does.

- Television *inhibits vocabulary development*. Even educational programs like *Sesame Street* are valuable only through the second grade. Reading develops vocabulary, not TV.
- TV has the *opposite effects of reading*; it serves to shorten the viewer's attention span and provides no time for reflection.
- TV is *anti-social*. A family watching television together is not really interacting; five people can spend hours together and barely speak. A child who watches TV extensively believes the characters are his "friends."
- TV viewers are *deprived of the opportunity to ask questions* through discussion.
- TV relies on *pictures and emotions* as opposed to reading and thinking. This stifles creativity and intellectual development.
- TV *stifles the imagination*, since nothing is left to the viewer's own creativity. At least in reading, children must imagine what the characters and sets look like. In writing or drawing, the imagination is fully active. This skill is important to develop for use in the child's future education, career, and personal life.
- In a Roper study several years ago, television was ranked as the number two cause for *family disharmony*. Many of us can relate to this, just in terms of who has possession of the remote control!
- TV creates a *false view of reality*. This is especially true with young children, who have not yet developed the ability to distinguish fantasy from real life. When they see the Roadrunner get smashed, then alive again a few minutes later, they become confused about mortality.
- Television *demands instant adulthood of children*, with shows on murder, rape, war, and violence (fighting is especially predominant in cartoons!). Kids are robbed of their innocence.

The *Medical Society Journal* suggests another detrimental effect:

> The primary danger of the television screen lies not so much in the behavior it produces, as the behavior it prevents.

As I briefly mentioned before, think about the activities our children miss out on by choosing to watch television:

- Reading.
- Talking about current events.
- Sports and activities.
- Child's play.
- Gardening.
- Homework.
- Responsibilities.
- Chores.
- Drawing and painting.
- Hobbies.
- Building things.
- Riding bikes.
- Hiking.
- Sewing.
- Family fun.
- Discussing theology or politics.

The list is almost endless. I think it all boils down to this: the effect on our children's future. *Memories are formed in real-life activities and experiences, not by television shows.*

> *Be very careful, then, how you live—not as unwise but as wise, making the most of every opportunity, because the days are evil.*
> (EPH. 5:15-16)

> *Set your minds on things above, not on earthly things.*
> (COL. 3:2)

These verses offer us some helpful advice, and it's good to ask ourselves what our minds are *set upon*. What are our own children's minds set upon? If they are watching television, what messages are they receiving? Is their focus on the Lord, or does television place their focus on earthly values, worldly ideas of success, and sin? Is this the best way to be "making the most of every opportunity" during our limited days on earth?

## GETTING CONTROL OF THE TELEVISION

How can you counteract the influence of the television and take control of this intrusion? Here are some helpful hints. I'm sure you've already come up with some good systems of your own.

1. Offer *yourself* in the TV's place. Your kids prefer spending time with you anyway!
2. Set up a viewing calendar (including computer games), setting a maximum of perhaps ten hours a week, with parental approval of selections. I've heard many different systems for controlling this. Here are a few:

- At the beginning of the week, go through the TV viewing guide together and determine what shows will be available and approved to watch.
- Buy a roll of "tickets" (like those used at carnivals or in raffles—available at party or paper goods stores), and give each child a weekly allowance of tickets, each good for one half hour of TV (approved viewing, only *after* homework and chores are completed).
- Keep a log of each child's viewing time and type of program, with only enough spaces to fill the allotted time.
- New products are coming onto the market to assist in limiting viewing. For example, "TimeSlot" is a box attached to the TV, through which each viewer must slide his own "viewing card." The box only allows a certain number of hours of viewing as programmed on the card (and I believe you can program it to accept the card only at certain times of the day).
- Remember to keep in mind that selection of programs is also important, and limitations need to be set and monitored. You may wish to develop an "approved list" of programs.

3. Watch at least *half* of what your child is viewing, so you can truly know what kinds of messages your child is receiving through each program.
4. Remember, you're the model! Are you a couch-potato yourself? Your child may follow suit.
5. "Out of sight, out of mind" bears consideration. If your television is kept in a cabinet rather than set prominently in the room, it doesn't come to mind as often. Also, children are less likely to watch if access is impaired; the more convenient the set is, the more it will be used. For example, if a child has his own TV in his bedroom, it is much more difficult for you to control. Also, if toys are kept in a separate playroom without a TV, children won't constantly have it on as "background noise" while they are playing.

6. In approving programming, I would suggest you obtain some of the excellent Christian children's video tapes available. For example, the "McGee & Me" series teaches morals to school-age children, and many excellent Christian cartoons (Hanna-Barbera and others) depict Bible stories. Many new products are coming out on the market; just watch a video product once to make sure you agree with it, then have it available for your children. These often become favorites.

7. Take full advantage of *family viewing times* by watching an educational program together, then discussing it and correcting any false information given.

8. I would suggest not using TV viewing as a reward. This practice places high value on television and sets it up as something to be desired. It's better to downplay the TV while making other activities sound much more fun and exciting.

9. When your children want to watch TV, ask them to first think of three other activities they could do instead. Perhaps they just haven't made the effort to come up with an idea that is more enjoyable. Just thinking about it may motivate them. Or you can suggest, "I thought you were just saying you really wanted to . . ."

10. Monitor your child's viewing at the homes of friends. This is more difficult but can be achieved through subtle questioning. Count this viewing time in their allotment, and try to know exactly what they are being exposed to.

## A WORD ON COMPUTER AND VIDEO GAMES

A discussion of television would not be complete without mentioning computer and video games. These activities also require time spent in front of a monitor. While such games can be used as valuable learning tools, utilizing strategy and coordination, there are many other activities that also develop these skills.

Time spent playing with *Nintendo* or other games should be counted as TV viewing time. I have a few of my own concerns about such games, which you may share. Many of the video games revolve around occultic fantasy, in the style of *Dungeons and Dragons*. Witches, warlocks, and spirits with demonic powers are utilized. The Bible repeatedly warns us to avoid any acceptance or involvement in the occult. While these games may just be "fantasy," I believe they may also be spiritually dangerous.

Parents are becoming concerned about the increasing violence in many video games and object to behavior changes observed in children after prolonged exposure to almost any computer or video game. Children often become obsessed with mastering a game or begin to act out the behavior of game characters.

Another concern is the prolonged exposure to Video Display Terminals (VDT's), which can be detrimental to a child's health. Robert A. Mendelson, immediate past chair of the American Academy of Pediatrics Committee on Communications, says there is no problem with children using computers for a short time each day. But "The combined time for a child to use a computer, watch TV and play video games should be limited to one to two hours daily. . . . Children should be doing active rather than passive activities for the remainder of the day."

We've all seen studies on health problems associated with extensive computer use by adults, including eye fatigue, skin rashes, and repetitive motion injuries like carpal-tunnel syndrome. As a writer who spends a great deal of time at my computer, I can certainly attest to my own headaches, eye strain, backaches, and arthritis! Surely, such dangers are also inherent in computer use by children.

Norma Miller, an environmental consultant to schools, cautions: "We do know that children are five to ten times more vulnerable to radiation than adults." If your children do use a home computer often, be sure it is set up correctly to minimize risks.

Robert L. Becker, a professor at the State University of New York Upstate Medical Center and an authority on the biological effects of electromagnetics, says that practical steps to mitigate field exposures during computer use are necessary since children are still growing and have a constant level of cell multiplication occurring in their bodies. A local computer store should be able to assist you.

Also, be aware of what your children are learning through interactive computer programs, especially those on topics such as decision-making and creativity. Some of these programs may not agree with your Christian values, directing students through a "values clarification" process that rejects parental authority or taking them on a New-Age-style "creative visualization" trip. Computer networks such as Internet can also provide a temptation to engage in ungodly opportunities such as pornography.

Staying on top of it all is the key to balance!

## Bringing It Home

*Applying God's Principles: Please refer to Chapter 2 for ideas on Family Night format and activities.*

**Opening:** Tonight we're going to talk about *television*. How much TV do you watch each day? (Write down each person's hours.) Why do you watch TV?

**Scripture:** Romans 8:5; Colossians 3:2; Ephesians 5:15-16.

**Discussion:** What kinds of shows do we watch on TV? What do they make us think about? Do they portray a Christian lifestyle or view of success? What kinds of things should we think about? How can we live as the wise and make "the most of every opportunity"?

**Application:** 1. Take out the paper where you wrote down how much TV each person estimated they watch a day. Add these figures together to get a daily family total. Then multiply by seven to see how many hours of TV your family watches a week. Now multiply that number by 52 to see how many hours of TV your family watches per year. Eye-opening, isn't it?

2. Discuss the meaning of this statement: "The primary danger of the television screen lies not so much in the behavior it produces, as the behavior it prevents." Think about happy memories. Do they involve TV programs or real activities? Which are *really* more fun?

3. Discuss how your family will regulate TV viewing, then follow through with action. Have each person list five things they would enjoy doing instead of watching TV. Keep the list for reference later.

# CHAPTER 12

◆

# *Teaching: Using Life as a Classroom*

As we all know, learning does not take place simply by osmosis. If it did, none of us would have needed to attend school. We would have learned to read simply by watching others do it and looking at words. We'd all become Bible scholars simply by holding the Word tightly to our chest and never actually reading it. Sometimes I wish this could be true, but unfortunately it isn't. Learning takes effort.

While modeling will have the greatest impact on our children's lives, since "actions speak louder than words," training is not complete without another important element: *teaching*.

There are many things you can teach a child: how to play baseball, how to cook, how to paint, history, grammar, foreign languages, gardening. The list is endless. In this book we will be focusing on four primary areas:

- Using life as a learning experience.
- Teaching wisdom and knowing God's will.
- Teaching your child to make good decisions.
- The importance of reading.

These four broad areas are of the greatest importance to your child's spiritual development. They essentially relate to virtually all other learning topics. And they fall under the realm and primary responsibility of home training.

I'm sure at least one reader is thinking, "But I send my children to school to learn. I'm not a teacher. The instructors at school are much more qualified than I am to teach my child. And whatever he misses at school, he'll pick up in Sunday school."

Just as we can't entrust *modeling* to our children's school or Sunday school teachers, who spend far less time with them than we do, neither can we neglect our responsibilities to *teach* our children at home. The Lord places these responsibilities squarely on our shoulders. We may choose to *delegate* some of those teaching and modeling duties to the school or the church, but we cannot abdicate our responsibility for our own children. Ultimately it is we, the parents, who must face the Lord and account for our children's training, including their teaching.

Remember, there are two primary disadvantages to delegating important instruction to your child's teachers:

1. The teacher is responsible for a classroom full of students—at least twenty, and perhaps as many as forty. He or she cannot give your child the necessary one-on-one attention that you can provide as a parent. Such personalized teaching provides an opportunity for vitally important *interaction*, as well as individual assistance, pacing, and monitoring of progress.
2. Another important consideration is values. Particularly if your child attends a public school, you need to be aware of the likelihood that the teacher does not share your Christian values; she may even feel antagonistic toward your beliefs. And even if your child is fortunate enough to have a Christian teacher, she cannot provide solid scriptural training on things like wisdom and knowing God's will because of laws governing the public schools.

The areas of teaching that we will cover in the next few chapters are especially important parts of home training, and they are easily integrated into the training model I have been presenting thus far.

## THE IMPORTANCE OF LEARNING

Think back to your high-school geometry class. Remember all those theorems you were taught? Can you still name the various shapes and calculate their areas? Could you apply this information today, in drawing up plans for a house?

Well, if you're an architect or engineer, you probably said, "Sure, no problem." Okay, why don't *you* try to recall your world history class. Can you remember the ancient cultures, their monetary systems, primary sources of trade, etc.? Probably not.

In fact, I'd venture to say that most of us could not pass the final tests in many high school or even junior high school classes if we were to take them right now. Why? Because we were *taught* a huge volume of information, but we only *learned* a small percentage of it. I know that is certainly true of myself. Why didn't I learn it all? I certainly knew the information at the time; in fact, I had straight A's. But I retained relatively little of it. It wasn't for lack of effort. I studied everything I was assigned, and I memorized it for the tests. But I remember, I *learned* only selected information.

Basically, to learn something, especially within the context of training that this book addresses, means to internalize a concept. Then it will not be forgotten; it can be taken out and used. Real learning can be applied in real-life situations. Many factors affect learning, but generally children learn best when the following conditions are present:

- The information is *relevant* to the student. The student is either interested in the topic or recognizes the usefulness or value it will contribute to his life.
- The information is *presented in a dynamic manner*. The learning is fun, interactive, or intriguing. The child participates in the learning rather than just having information presented to him.
- Learning is reinforced through *repetition*. If you're teaching a child to hit the ball with a bat, you know the child must practice. He won't learn if you simply illustrate the technique and then let him try it one time. This same principle results in children doing worksheets of math problems; they are practicing the skill of, say, multiplying. It also applies to skills like learning from the Bible and decision-making.
- The information must be *explained*. Children will learn better if they understand why it is necessary to know the information or perform the skill, if they recognize how they can apply it to real-life situations, and if they clearly understand the information or process that is being conveyed. In other words, they must know why, how, what, and when.
- Finally, they must *accept* what is being taught. This principle can work for you or against you. For example, if you've clearly taught

your child the biblical facts of creation, then your child will refuse to accept the theory of evolution when it is taught at school. He may learn *about* evolution (which is helpful in discussing creation with evolutionists), but he won't internalize the teacher's instruction and believe evolution to be a fact. On the other hand, our children will not accept what we teach them about integrity if they see us lying (our model will speak louder than our instruction).

As we set forth on the path of teaching our children, we must keep these principles in mind. Everything we teach them should be relevant, dynamic, repeated, explained, and acceptable (because it is consistent with what they see and know already). In this way we can insure that our children will *learn* what we teach them.

## TEACHING YOUR CHILD HOW TO THINK

Another key element of teaching, but an often overlooked one, is the importance of teaching our children *how* to think, not simply *what* to think. As we all grow older, we encounter more and more situations in which we must decide what we think. And often these are new, uncharted areas where no one has ever *told* us what to think.

Perhaps you were young when the Vietnam War was going on. Your feelings on the war were likely developed in large part by what other people (perhaps your parents or teachers) told you to think about the war. If you were a child, you probably did not carefully evaluate all aspects of the war and form an opinion all on your own. You took the cue of someone you trusted.

But now you are faced with news accounts of military actions around the globe. A while ago you had to form an opinion on the Gulf War. Tough issues, aren't they? Did you simply follow what someone else told you to think about the Gulf War? Now that you're an adult, you probably approached it in somewhat the same manner as I did. I asked the opinion of people with experience and wisdom. I also read extensively about the issue. I watched news accounts. I observed round-table debates with experts on both sides of the issue. I prayed about it. Then, taking all the facts into consideration, I formed my own opinion—an opinion I could defend and explain since I'd formed it on my own.

When we were young we could get by in life by going on what someone else told us to think. But once we're on our own, we must know *how* to think if we are to survive. The skill of knowing how to think is needed daily—not just in forming political opinions, but in deciding which long distance company to select, getting the best value for your dollar when you shop, being careful so you don't get robbed, raising your children, discerning God's will, and making moral decisions.

One of the best gifts we can give our children is to teach them how to think for themselves. In the day in which we live, this is especially important at even very young ages. We can no longer trust that schools will uphold our traditional family values and the Judeo-Christian ethic. We can no longer allow our children to trust strangers or believe what anyone in authority tells them. Kidnappers and child molesters pose as policemen to lure our children away. Teachers hold some very strange ideas, and some seek to subvert the authority of parents. We live in scary times, and more than ever our children need to gain wisdom and learn how to think!

## THE ESSENTIAL NATURE OF THE MIND

The Bible emphasizes the importance of our mind, our intellect, and the way in which we use it. Proverbs 23:7 (KJV) tells us:

*For as he thinketh in his heart, so is he . . .*

What we think, will show itself in our lifestyle. I am what I think. As we develop a godly mind-set, it will change our character—the optimal condition under which to train our children. When we focus our thoughts on the Lord, our lives will be focused on Him as well, and we will be better models. We can also help our children to think upon things of the Lord and think *like* the Lord by teaching them the wisdom of the Word. This will shape their character. So, the first reason the mind is important is:

• Our thoughts shape our character.

Paul said Christians are given the mind of Christ. Therefore, we should take advantage of the abilities and discernment He gives us, so that we might have knowledge and wisdom and know right from wrong.

If a child does not learn how to think carefully and evaluate all he (or she) is told, he will not recognize the false teachings to which he will be exposed throughout life—on television, in the newspaper, at school, or when a cult recruiter approaches him. Helping our children develop a godly mind-set will enable them to make good decisions and distinguish godly from ungodly teaching.

It is so sad to see Christians accept humanistic worldviews on moral issues like homosexuality or abortion. If we are not grounded in the Word, God's truth, we can be fooled by the arguments of the world. Humanistic arguments often look good on the surface; and when combined with social pressure to think in a "politically correct" manner, it is easy for unthinking Christians to just go with the flow and adopt what they are *told* to think rather than seeing the issue through God's eyes and thinking with discernment that seeks out the biblical viewpoint.

Therefore, the second reason for teaching your child to use his or her mind is:

• Having the mind of Christ protects us from false teaching.

Missionary-evangelist Stanley Jones illustrates the essential nature of the mind in relation to the way we love God:

> The Christian position is "Thou shalt love the Lord thy God with all thy mind"—the intellectual nature; "with all thy heart"—the emotional nature; "with all thy soul"—the willing nature; and "with all thy strength"—the physical nature. The total person is to love him—mind, emotion, will, strength. But the "strength" might mean the strength of all three. Some love him with the strength of the mind and the weakness of emotion—the intellectualist in religion; some love him with the strength of emotion and the weakness of the mind—the sentimentalist in religion; some love him with the strength of the will and the weakness of emotion—the man of iron who is not very approachable. But loving God with the strength of the mind, the strength of the emotion, and the strength of the will—that makes the truly Christian and truly balanced and truly strong character. (*Song of Ascents* [Nashville: Abingdon, 1968], p. 189, quoted in Gordon MacDonald, *Ordering Your Private World* [Nashville: Oliver-Nelson, 1985])

Thus, a well-developed mind or godly intellect allows us to worship and serve the Lord with greater strength and a well-balanced Christian character. This provides us with the third reason why the mind is essential:

• A well-developed mind is essential to a truly strong, balanced, Christian character.

Interestingly, Jones also contrasts this Christian position with the view (found in the New Age movement and other religions) that one must empty the mind for meditation, an activity in which many public schools ask children to participate. When the mind is empty, Satan loves to fill the void. God tells us to meditate, or think upon, what is good and pure and holy. Surely, meditating upon God's goodness will better accomplish the purpose of "relaxation" than will an "empty" mind!

## KNOWING HOW TO THINK

Just how do we teach our children how to think? One way is to teach them good decision-making skills. We'll cover exactly how to do this in an upcoming chapter. Another way is to instill wisdom in them and teach them how to discern the will of God. We'll discuss ways to do that in the next chapter. But foundational for both decision-making and wisdom is knowledge of the Bible.

Teaching our children how to think begins with grounding them in the Word. When they are very small, we can read Bible stories to them, discussing how the Bible characters decided what to do in certain situations and showing them how Jesus used His intellect to think about things and do what was right (for instance, when Satan offered him the three temptations in the wilderness).

As our children get older, we can help them develop the discipline of spending time in the Word daily. We can also reinforce these lessons through Family Nights and discussions that occur over meals, while driving, or as part of our daily lives.

How does the Bible tell us we should develop our thinking skills?

*But test everything that is said to be sure it is true, and if it is, then accept it.*

(1 THESS. 5:21, TLB)

If we can teach our children to "test everything that is said," they will be protected from falling victim to the false teachings of the world and of cults. Isn't that wonderful? But how do they test everything that is said?

*Bless me with life so that I can continue to obey you. Open my eyes to see wonderful things in your Word. I am but a pilgrim here on earth: how I need a map—and your commands are my chart and guide. I long for your instructions more than I can tell.*

(Ps. 119:17-20, TLB)

Through the Bible, God has provided us with everything we need to make it through life. His Word is a map. God's commands are a chart and a guide to lead us through the stormy waters of life. His Word teaches us how to think by providing us with models of righteous men and women to follow and by giving us principles to observe when we form opinions, discern right from wrong, and make choices.

While the Bible may not give us specific answers to every question we have, it does provide us with every principle we need to make a correct judgement on our own.

For instance, my husband and I are currently deciding upon what type of life insurance to purchase. The Bible doesn't say, "Term-life is better," or "Buy universal-life insurance instead of whole-life." And it doesn't tell us which companies are more stable than others. But it does give us principles that guide our thinking. The Bible talks extensively about financial stewardship, our responsibilities to our family members, and principles of usury. From this guide, we were able to make a decision on what is best for our family.

Now, the life insurance policy best for our family may not be the best for your family. Such decisions are complicated, involving health, age, financial position, future financial capabilities, assets, and more. Every family has different circumstances that weigh into such a complex decision.

I think this may be why the Bible doesn't simply tell us *what* to think but teaches us *how* to think. In this way, God has allowed us the flexibility to factor in various circumstances, such as those that determine life insurance needs. Yet the Lord clearly directs us in the overriding principles. Isn't the Bible a wonderful guide? By God's special design, it applies to every person, despite our diversity, through all time!

## USING THE WORD AS YOUR GUIDE

When our children learn the principles of the Bible and make those truths part of their lives, they will be protected.

> *Blessed is the man . . . [whose] delight is in the law of the Lord, and on his law he meditates day and night.*
> (Ps. 1:1-2)

> *For the Lord watches over the way of the righteous, but the way of the wicked will perish.*
> (Ps. 1:6)

Your child will be blessed by meditating upon the Word day and night. Does this mean you should shove it down her throat and lock her in her room until she memorizes the Bible? Of course not.

I don't believe the Lord intends for us to force our children to sit in their rooms day and night reading the Bible. In fact, shoving it down their throats could have the opposite effect of what we really desire. I think God wants us to impress His truths upon our children in a natural way, by making Him the center of our lives and our families. We can easily incorporate discussions of godly principles and what the Bible says as activities naturally occur throughout the day and evening. The Lord instructed the Israelites to:

> *Fix these words of mine in your hearts and minds; tie them as symbols on your hands and bind them on your foreheads. Teach them to your children, talking about them when you sit at home and when you walk along the road, when you lie down and when you get up.*

(DEUT. 11:18-19)

## USING LIFE AS A CLASSROOM

In that last passage, God is basically telling us to use life as a classroom. Make His Word, His instruction, part of your daily life, and use every opportunity to teach your children His truth.

We must write God's *truth* upon our children's hearts, so that they will be able to discern false teaching that they encounter in the public schools, in society (TV, friends, etc.), and even in churches. Many false teachings are presented to our children each day, including:

- Evolution is a "fact," proving there is no God.
- New-Age ideas that we are our own god are unquestionable.
- Perversions such as homosexuality are acceptable.
- The devaluing of life by abortion and euthanasia is okay.
- Premarital sex and affairs are allowable; just have "safe" sex.
- Drugs are common; just use them carefully and in moderation.
- You are more important than anything or anyone else.
- Most problems and weaknesses can be blamed on someone else—society or your parents, for example.
- Violence is a necessary part of life.
- You must be rich to be happy.
- You must accept all others' ideas and respect their behavior if you are truly tolerant.

- The environment is more important than people.
- We must form a fully global society if we are to survive.

The list is endless and false teaching pervasive. What can we as parents do to counteract this false teaching?

Do you know how bank tellers are trained to spot counterfeit money? One might logically suppose they are exposed to the fake and taught to recognize it. But actually the opposite is true. They are constantly exposed to real currency until, when someone tries to pass a counterfeit bill, they can easily distinguish the fake because it doesn't seem or feel quite right.

We can protect our children from false teaching in the same way. Yes, there is value in exposing wrong when you see it, explaining why it is false, and contrasting it with the truth. It is important, however, that the child doesn't begin to focus on looking for the fake to the point that his primary exposure is detracted from the purity of the truth. The best strategy is to immerse your child in God's truth and wisdom, so that when counterfeit teaching comes along he or she will have no trouble discerning it.

> *But solid food is for the mature, who by constant use have trained themselves to distinguish good from evil.*
> (HEB. 5:14)

This is a biblical concept! The Scripture tells us to constantly use "solid food"—that is, God's truth. A steady diet of Scripture and solid Christian teaching will expose our children to the real thing so pervasively that false teaching from society or public schools will be easily recognizable.

Life offers us so many opportunities to teach our children. We just need to consciously search for these opportunities throughout the day and share them with our kids. In fact, you probably already do this without even realizing it. Most of us feel like praising the Lord at some time during the day, perhaps when a thought occurs to us or an observation is made. Take time to share this insight or praise with your child. Here are some examples:

- Nature is a source of knowledge. God reveals Himself to us daily in the miracle of life and creation all around us. Take the time to marvel at the clouds, the immensity of the universe, or the multitude of stars. How enormous is our God to hold all that in His hand! Or if you know someone who is pregnant, discuss the miracle of how a mother's body changes to accommodate and nurture the baby, then returns to its normal function after birth. Only our Lord could create such a magnificent and specialized system! The Bible says:

> *The heavens declare the glory of God; the skies proclaim the work of his hands. Day after day they pour forth speech; night after night they display knowledge.*
>
> (Ps. 19:1-2)

- Children have a natural curiosity, especially when they are younger. Instead of getting frustrated by the multitude of questions—especially the tough ones we can't answer!—we can use these opportunities to teach. When a question comes up, like "Why do the leaves change colors in the fall?" or "What makes the noise of thunder?" we can consult our handy-dandy encyclopedia and search out the answer together with our child. This exercise not only answers the question (and teaches Mom or Dad something new!), but it also teaches the child *how to find answers*, a vitally important part of learning.

- There are many ways to teach your children how to make decisions. First, you can begin to let them make some decisions for themselves, as is appropriate to their age level. Allow choices within parentally-set limits. For example, a five-year-old girl, left to choose anything she wants to wear out of her closet, is likely to choose an outfit inappropriate for the occasion or the weather. But she'll probably be just as happy and proud of her decision if you select several appropriate choices and let her pick her favorite.

- Another important decision-making tool is modeling. As you make a family decision—for example, on where to vacation—allow everyone to take part and "talk through" your thought process. Brainstorm several ideas; then eliminate poorer choices based on expense, time, and weather factors. Let the kids help research this information to help with the decision. Then, of those choices remaining, examine the activities and accommodations available and make a family choice.

- When difficult decisions must be made, take it to the Lord in prayer as a family. Together, search the Bible for biblical principles to guide you.

- Thinking aloud is a great tool for teaching. Even as you go grocery shopping with a smaller child, explain why you are buying one brand over another, based on quality or price. As the child gets older, let him or her help make the decision by comparing price and quantity to determine the best value.

- Teach your child financial responsibility by sitting down together to determine an appropriate allowance, what the child's responsibilities will be to obtain the allowance, and what she will need to budget for purchases. For example, when I was young I received a small allowance for doing chores around the house. I could spend the money however I wanted to, after I tithed to the Sunday school offering. As I got older I was given a larger allowance, but I had to buy most of my own clothes out of it and pay for entertainment and eating out with friends. My parents helped me set up a budget, using envelopes and a ledger, to make sure I didn't run out of cash before I needed it. With this system I learned to be financially responsible and independent, and I had no problems at all when I moved into my first apartment and supported myself.

- As you teach budgeting, it is helpful to expose your children to the family budget. While being careful not to lay the financial burdens of the family upon the shoulders of your children, this is a great way to expose them to the reality of the cost of living and to help them understand priorities and limitations, as well as the importance of planning and budgeting. Don't forget to teach them the importance of saving and tithing (which should come from their *heart*).

- Large purchases provide another great opportunity to teach your children. For example, when buying a house, a car, or an appliance, let your child follow along through the process. This experience will be helpful to them later in life when they face similar needs. Discuss the decision-making process, evaluating quality and performance, warranties, options, etc., and model the way you seek God's will and pray about the decision.

This also offers a great opportunity to teach them about debt. Can we afford the debt? How can we get the best interest rate, or several months interest free? How much will this item *really* cost before it's paid for? What if something happens to the item before it's paid for? Do we need insurance? What will the payments be? Can we pay it off faster by paying extra toward the principal? What is our debt/income ratio? Is this an appreciating or depreciating item?

I remember when my dad took my brother, Ross, shopping for motorcycles. They wanted two dirt bikes, and there were many wonderful options to choose from. Of course, eleven-year-old Ross wanted a top-of-the-line, brand-new model. But they looked at all the options, found two at a garage sale that were in great shape and inexpensive, and bought them with cash. The value of the lesson: you don't always have to buy the *best,* just the *best value.*

- There are many excellent Christian books on how to teach your child character traits through everyday activities. Also, the U.S. Department of Education offers several booklets for parents on teaching, including one called *Helping Your Child Get Ready for School* that contains "life lessons" in activities and projects. For information on ordering and availability, call the U.S. Government Printing Office Order Desk at (202) 783-3238. Ask for GPO stock #065-000-00522-1 and a list of booklets for parents.
- Chores can be a great source of learning, and they also help the child to develop a sense of responsibility. Chores can be made more fun and interesting by having quality contests, races for who does their chores earliest in the day or week, etc. The prize may be Mom's fixing the child's favorite dinner or some other special recognition.

## HELPING YOUR CHILD LEARN BETTER AT SCHOOL

Whether our children attend public or private school, as parents we must always remember that we are partners in teaching. To be effective, schools need parental support of learning at home. In addition to biblical and character training, we can help with schoolwork by enforcing homework standards and completion, responsible planning on long-term assignments, and development of a positive attitude toward learning.

Children learn best when what they are learning is meaningful. You can help make their schoolwork meaningful and make homework and projects more enjoyable by offering your enthusiasm, assistance, and encouragement. You can help them set long- and short-term goals, so their schoolwork does not become a last-minute pressure. Good friends, who see school as important, and parental interest greatly affect a child's attitude toward learning. Staying in close contact with your child's teacher is a great way to help your child. Ask the teacher to keep you aware of your child's strengths and weaknesses, and also areas where the child may need extra support and encouragement. Also, review all your child's curricula yourself, so you'll be aware of potential problems and opportunities. It's helpful to ask your child's teacher some questions a couple of times a year. For example, ask them to rate your child, on a scale of 1 (not true) to 7 (very true), on the following characteristics:

- My child's schoolwork is neat and legible.
- My child completes his/her projects.
- My child keeps up with his/her daily tasks.
- My child completes his/her homework on time.
- My child is organized at school.
- My child takes pride in the quality of his/her work.
- My child is motivated to achieve.
- My child enjoys learning.
- My child handles challenging work well.
- My child is confident in his/her ability to learn.
- My child is not easily discouraged.
- My child expects to succeed.
- My child has mastered the basics of writing.
- My child has mastered the basics of reading.
- My child has mastered the basics of mathematics.
- My child's interests are balanced and well-rounded.
- My child is helpful to others.

You may wish to periodically complete the above evaluation (adapted as needed) on your child at home as well, for your own information. Those skills that are lacking can be encouraged and practiced, and those present can be praised.

A student should be able to answer *why* he or she is in a particular class. Often young people never think about why they go to school. To that question they might respond, "Because I have to" or "Because I want to get a job." Both of these reasons are insufficient motivators. An important job we hold as parents is to motivate our children by helping them to understand why it is important and valuable to each child personally to learn each subject they study in school. We can help do this by showing them how the knowledge can be used in real life. For instance, if your child is learning algebra, ask them a question about price comparisons; then show them how to use an algebraic equation to find the answer. Of if your child is studying art, take her to the museum for inspiration. Use a news broadcast or a local election to help your child apply his civics lessons; ask him his opinion on a candidate or issue.

We have a wonderful opportunity to use the world as a learning tool while remaining firmly rooted in God's truth. Or we can drift through life, letting the world use us, manipulating and warping our beliefs, if our footing lacks a firm foundation and we fail to have a proactive plan. It's up to us to take the reins, anchor ourselves to the Word, and learn from the world within the protective screen of godliness, rather than letting the sin of the world corrupt and compromise us. Life is an endless classroom, just waiting to be used!

## Bringing It Home

*Applying God's Principles: Please refer to Chapter 2 for ideas on Family Night format and activities.*

**Opening:** Why is learning important? Where do we learn things?

**Scripture:** 1 Timothy 6:20-21; Titus 1:9.

**Discussion:** How is the knowledge of the world different from the truth of the Bible? Why is it important to read the Bible, God's Word, and know what it says? Discuss some ways in which the false knowledge of the world conflicts with the truth of the Bible (i.e., evolution or the New Age). Which is more reliable, the Bible or science?

**Application:** 1. When Christ was in the desert being tempted by Satan for forty days, He used Scripture to refute Satan's lies (see Luke 4:1-13). How can you use the Word as an arsenal of weapons, like Christ did, to fight the influence of false messages you hear?

2. Read Titus 1:9 again, replacing "he" with your own name. Why should you hide the Word in your heart and use it? How can you use it at school? Ephesians 6:13-18 tells us to put on the whole armor of God. Why is this important for your life?

3. Each person should decide on one way to begin growing in godly knowledge, either through reading the Bible, listening to tapes, or memorizing verses. Begin this week.

# CHAPTER 13

◆

# *Teaching Wisdom and Knowing God's Will*

I f God offered to give you whatever you wanted, what would you ask for? Solomon had this very experience. First Kings 3:5 tells us that God said to him, "Ask for whatever you want me to give you." Solomon asked for the ability to know right from wrong and judge rightly because his father, David, had impressed upon him the great importance of wisdom, saying:

> Wisdom is supreme; therefore get wisdom. Though it cost all you have,
> get understanding.
>
> (PROV. 4:7)

As parents, it is important for us, too, to seek wisdom and to impress upon our children the importance of wisdom and knowledge. Wisdom will give them discerning hearts and minds, able to distinguish right from wrong, so that by your good training they will automatically do what is right. When our children become wise, they will see the value of a righteous life, and they will be protected from temptation.

## WHY WISDOM IS IMPORTANT

Our families should place the utmost importance upon the pursuit of wisdom for many reasons. First of all, Scripture tells us that *wisdom is precious* and that we should seek it out. In fact, the Bible says nothing compares with it. That means wisdom is more important than any worldly knowledge, than any skill, than any gift or possession.

> *Choose my instruction instead of silver, knowledge rather than choice gold, for wisdom is more precious than rubies, and nothing you desire can compare with her.*
> (PROV. 8:10-11)

> *How much better to get wisdom than gold, to choose understanding rather than silver.*
> (PROV. 16:16)

Wisdom comes linked with understanding and knowledge. If we are wise, we will be able to discern what is right from what is wrong and to do what is right. Wisdom will help us be more godly and better serve the Lord; that makes it infinitely precious and greatly to be desired.

*Power and strength* also result from wisdom.

> *A wise man has great power, and a man of knowledge increases strength.*
> (PROV. 24:5)

Being wise and knowing we are in God's will gives us tremendous confidence and power, for no one can defeat our Lord; His truth is supreme. There is power in the blood of Christ; and if we follow Him, we cannot fail. Our strength is in the Lord.

The confidence we have in His power and strength working through us is just one of the many *blessings* that comes from wisdom. Imagine all the pitfalls in the life of someone who lacks wisdom and makes one mistake after another. If we seek the Lord's wisdom and act upon it, we are spared those mistakes and instead experience the blessings that come from obeying Him.

> *Blessed is the man who finds wisdom, the man who gains understanding.*
> (PROV. 3:13)

Among the blessings of wisdom are the many *moral benefits* it will bring to your children. Proverbs 2:1–22 lists many of these benefits, saying that wisdom, the knowledge of what's right, will:

- Help them understand the fear of the Lord and find the knowledge of God.
- Act as a shield and bring victory to the blameless.
- Protect and guard them.
- Save them from wicked men and women.
- Bring righteousness (*doing* what's right in addition to *knowing* what's right).

For these reasons, the Bible commands us:

*Buy the truth and do not sell it; get wisdom, discipline and understanding.*
(PROV. 23:23)

But wait, there's more! Your children even get the added bonus of higher school achievement. A 1993 *USA Today*/CNN/Gallup poll suggests that religious students are more likely to succeed in school, earning mostly A's and enjoying school more. Obviously, the Lord's wisdom has practical applications too!

## THE PURSUIT OF REAL WISDOM

Many people in this world believe they are wise, including many who do not know the Lord. But do they have real wisdom? How do you know if your family is truly wise?

The Bible lists many specific characteristics of wisdom. First of all, true wisdom comes from the Lord. In fact, it *begins* with the fear of the Lord. That alone eliminates non-Christians.

*The fear of the Lord is the beginning of knowledge, but fools despise wisdom and discipline.*
(PROV. 1:7)

*The fear of the Lord is the beginning of wisdom, and knowledge of the Holy One is understanding.*
(PROV. 9:10)

To be wise, we must fear the Lord. We must reverence Him and stand in awe of His glorious nature, understanding who we are in relationship to the magnitude of who He is. I fear the Lord by recognizing His holiness and praising and worshiping Him. I realize that He knows me more intimately than I know myself, and He is sovereign in my life. What is fearing the Lord all about? Not being "afraid" of Him, but honoring His power and love.

We must teach our children to fear the Lord if we desire for them to be wise. Earlier we discussed this in more detail in the chapter on "Our Identity in Christ."

Fearing the Lord is the beginning of knowledge and wisdom, but notice the link, in Proverbs 1:7, to "discipline." Self-control and self-discipline must accompany wisdom. Sadly, Solomon lacked self-control; so wisdom alone wasn't enough to protect him from temptation and the tragedy that sin brought to his life. Self-control must guide our actions, and we must discipline ourselves to constantly seek wisdom and understanding in God's Word and through prayer and obedience.

To be wise, our children must be righteous. That is, they must act upon their knowledge of right and wrong. A man who knows what is right, yet chooses to sin is no better than a man who is ignorant or rejects God's commands.

> *The mouth of the righteous brings forth wisdom, but a perverse tongue will be cut out.*
> (PROV. 10:31)

> *For the wisdom of this world is foolishness in God's sight. As it is written: "He catches the wise in their craftiness...."*
> (1 COR. 3:19)

Remember, true wisdom is from the Lord, and only the righteous can be wise. God has no interest in the supposed "wisdom" of the world.

To fear the Lord and be righteous, we must read His Word. Understanding comes from a knowledge of God.

> *Remember what Christ taught and let his words enrich your lives and make you wise.*
> (COL. 3:16, TLB)

Remember, the Word is sufficient for all instruction. The Bible is full of nuggets of wisdom, principles to live by, and godly models of righteousness. All we have to do is read it and follow it. Paul's letters alone reflect the daily practicalities of Christ's teachings, which, if we are wise, we will apply to our own lives.

The Bible is meant to *help* us, train us, and guide us, not to inflict guilt or exert pressure. Christ came to *free* us. I really encourage you to get your child a Bible version that will be understandable to his or her age level; there are great products on the market specifically geared to children and teens—even picture books for non-readers!

The wisdom that comes from God, which our families strive for, is easily distinguishable from the wisdom of the world by its attitude as well as by its source.

> *But the wisdom that comes from heaven is first of all pure; then peace loving, considerate, submissive, full of mercy and good fruit, impartial and sincere.*
>
> (JAS. 3:17)

Those are the attitudes that will be prevalent in wise Christian homes. When we looked at the atmosphere we wanted in our families, weren't these the very same characteristics? If we are wise, we will be successful. Personally, I'd say that seeing the presence of these characteristics in my children is reason enough to train them in wisdom.

Notice that wisdom bears "good fruit." Wisdom is not just internal knowledge or external attitudes. Like success, it requires obedient action, doing what is right—*and* doing it with the right attitude.

> *When pride comes, then comes disgrace, but with humility comes wisdom.*
>
> (PROV. 11:2)

Just as when we do good it is easy to feel self-righteous, when we are wise it is easy to feel proud. But when we do good *for others and for the Lord*, our reward comes later, not in public recognition. Wisdom comes from the Lord, by His instruction and grace, not by our own intelligence. Wisdom has nothing to do with IQ. We can boast only in the Lord.

> *This is what the Lord says: "Let not the wise man boast of his wisdom or the strong man boast of his strength or the rich man boast of his riches, but let him who boasts boast about this: that he understands and*

*knows me, that I am the* LORD, *who exercises kindness, justice and righteousness on the earth, for in these I delight," declares the* LORD.
(JER. 9:23-24)

## HOW TO BECOME WISE

To sum up its characteristics, real wisdom:

- Begins with the fear of the Lord.
- Must be accompanied by discipline and self-control.
- Resides in the righteous, not the worldly.
- Is found in the Bible.
- Breeds godly attitudes.
- Bears good fruit.
- Is humble.

So how can we attain wisdom, and how can our children gain wisdom? First, and most importantly, wisdom is found in the Word of God. We must be firmly grounded in God's truth and instruct our children in the knowledge of the Scriptures.

*And how from infancy you have known the holy Scriptures, which are able to make you wise for salvation through faith in Christ Jesus.*
(2 TIM. 3:15)

It's never too early to start teaching your children Bible stories and exposing them to biblical principles. Once they are immersed in God's Word, they will be able to apprehend the mind of Christ, as Philippians 2:5 instructs. When we model Christ and study His life in the Scriptures, we become better able to think like He thinks and in fact become more like Him. Undoubtedly, Jesus Christ was the wisest, most successful man to walk the earth, for He is the Lord.

If we truly seek wisdom, we will find it, for Jesus tells us that if we are in His Word and He is in our lives, He will answer our call.

*"If you remain in me and my words remain in you, ask whatever you wish, and it will be given you."*
(JOHN 15:7)

I constantly pray and ask the Lord to give me wisdom and to reveal His truth to me as I read the Bible each day. He answers my prayers and gives me understanding where I need it! Walking with the

Lord is the best way to become wise, and it is also helpful to keep the company of other wise people, other successful Christians.

> *He who walks with the wise grows wise, but a companion of fools suffers harm.*
>
> (PROV. 13:20)

Becoming wise really isn't that hard, is it? All we have to do is fear the Lord, have self-control and a humble attitude in using wisdom, ask the Lord for it, associate with godly friends, and, finally, know the will of God.

## HOW TO KNOW GOD'S WILL

Knowing God's will and wisdom walk hand in hand. If you are wise, you will be able to *discern* God's will. If you are wise, you will act upon that wisdom and *do* God's will. Living our lives in accordance with God's desires makes us successful.

How can we know God's will for our own lives and for our families? It's really not difficult. God reveals His will to us in many ways; we just need to search for it.

Sometimes it is truly miraculous the way God reveals His plan, and I just bask in His presence, knowing that He is working in my life in a mighty way. My husband and I recently had this experience in buying our first home. We hadn't even started seriously looking yet and didn't plan to for at least another month. But God's timing is always perfect, and He knew best what we needed.

We had been praying for years that He would provide us with just the right house, if it was His will that we buy one, at just the right time. Over the past year He had brought us to a new area of the state, placed my husband in a new job, placed us in a new church and circle of friends, and blessed us with a child that will be born in the spring. Now we are in escrow on a house that is just ideal for us and very affordable, and the entire process has gone very smoothly—that's a miracle in itself.

We have sought scriptural principles in the Bible, sought the counsel of godly people we respect (including my parents), and prayed a great deal for guidance. God led us to the perfect house, at an amazing price, and arranged financing in a miraculous way we never would have found ourselves. Every circumstance has confirmed His perfect plan, and all those involved in the transaction are Christians whom we didn't know before.

In fact, our offer was accepted with no changes (another miracle), and the owner of the house had informed his daughter-in-law a week earlier that the Lord told him in prayer that a Christian couple would buy the house for exactly the amount we offered. All he asked the real estate agent was whether or not we were Christians! What a blessing to see God work in such a powerful way, beyond any possibility of coincidence, and to be part of His plan! We've been praising Him continuously!

The Lord has a plan for each of us. Psalm 37:23, KJV says:

> The steps of a good man are ordered by the Lord: and he delighteth in his way.

He loves to make plans for us, and He wants to reveal them to us!

> Therefore don't be foolish, but understand what the Lord's will is.
> (EPH. 5:17)

God wants us to be wise and to know His will, then to be "doing the will of God from your heart" (Eph. 6:6). Exactly how can we search for His will? He reveals it in five key areas:

- *Prayer.* If you want to know God's will, ask Him to reveal it to you! And then *listen.* Be still and know that He is God. Have your Bible ready in case He directs your mind to certain Scriptures. If you want to know your spouse's thoughts, you ask him or her, right? Well, ask God specifically for help, and be in constant prayer for general direction in your life. Then obey what He tells you, even if it's not the answer you were looking for or hoping He'd give.

  > Trust in the Lord with all your heart and lean not on your own understanding; in all your ways acknowledge him, and he will make your paths straight.
  > (PROV. 3:5-6)

- *Scripture.* Seek the Lord's will in specific cases and on a continual basis. For specific situations, use a concordance (there may be one in the back of your Bible, and many are available at a local Christian bookstore) to search out key words and topics that apply to your situation. Also, regularly read your Bible. He will reveal things when you aren't even looking for them!

> *Do not conform any longer to the pattern of this world, but be transformed by the renewing of your mind. Then you will be able to test and approve what God's will is—his good, pleasing and perfect will.*
> (ROM. 12:2)

- *Godly counsel.* Seek the wise advice of Christians you trust, those who, by the fruit of their lives and their integrity and prayer lives, walk closely with the Lord. It is particularly helpful to consult those who are not personally involved with your situation; they will have more objectivity and will tell you what's *right* rather than what they know you want to hear. Remember, your counselors are human and make mistakes; so have several advisors.

> *Blessed is the man who does not walk in the counsel of the wicked or stand in the way of sinners or sit in the seat of mockers.*
> (PS. 1:1)

Walk in the counsel of the godly, not the wicked!

> *Wisdom is found on the lips of the discerning.*
> (PROV. 10:13)

> *. . . many advisors make victory sure.*
> (PROV. 11:14)

- *Circumstances.* While this is the least important means of discerning God's will, it often provides confirmation of what you already believe His will to be, based on searching the other areas. But be careful—Satan can open doors too and can use circumstances to mislead you.
- *Think.* God gave us brains and intelligence for a reason. He also gives us wisdom, if we seek it and walk in His paths. The Lord intends for us to *use* our wisdom and intelligence to make godly decisions.

Finally, if God opens a door, He'll keep it open. He has plenty of time; in fact, time doesn't even exist in heaven. If you're trying to make a decision, don't let someone pressure you by saying things like "The deal is only good this week" or "Another buyer is coming in tonight."

If it's God's will for you to make the purchase or accept the offer, it will still be there when you are ready and feel certain of God's direction. If it's not there, it wasn't meant to be. This is especially important to teach children, since they are especially susceptible to pressure tactics. I like to remember the catchy phrase, which I've heard said many times: "God leads, Satan pushes!"

## Bringing It Home

*Applying God's Principles: Please refer to Chapter 2 for ideas on Family Night format and activities.*

**Opening:** What does it mean to be wise? Do you want to be wise? Why?

**Scripture:** Proverbs 1:7-9; Proverbs 3 (shorten for younger children).

**Discussion:** Why should you listen to your parents? How do you become wise? (See Prov. 1:7-9.)

**Application:**
1. As a family, go through Proverbs 3 and list the benefits of wisdom.

2. Proverbs 3:2 says wisdom will prolong your life. How can it do that? (Example: it will protect you from sin that can kill you—AIDS from fornication, etc.)

3. What actions does wisdom require? (Example: living righteously; self-control; doing God's will.)

4. If you need to know God's will for a specific situation in your family, seek it right now through prayer, the Bible, etc. Or discuss an example of how you've sought His will in the past or will do so in the future. Why is knowing God's will important?

5. What's one thing you can do this week to become wiser?

# CHAPTER 14

♦

# *Teaching Good Decision-making*

Children who are on automatic pilot will make good decisions. They develop stock answers to difficult moral dilemmas. Equipping our children with God's wisdom is the first step toward helping them become good decision-makers.

> *You know how, when you were a small child, you were taught the holy Scriptures; and it is these that make you wise to accept God's salvation by trusting in Christ Jesus. The whole Bible was given to us by inspiration from God and is useful to teach us what is true and to make us realize what is wrong in our lives; it straightens us out and helps us do what is right. It is God's way of making us well prepared at every point, fully equipped to do good to everyone.*
>
> (2 TIM. 3:15-17, TLB)

Wisdom, from the Bible, is the best protection available to our children. It's also important for parents to recognize the outright efforts of the world to *prevent* our children from making godly decisions. It's also important for our children to be able to identify the falsity of such worldly thought processes and to have a positive, godly, alternative strategy for making good decisions.

Children are exposed to worldly values through a wide array of media, including television, music, movies, books, peers, and especially public schools. When public schools began in this country, the

Bible was used as a textbook, and scriptural standards of right and wrong were upheld and reinforced. Since then, there has been a tragic drift toward progressive education and humanistic values. Classroom standards of right and wrong have taken on a more "relative nature." Values clarification and situation ethics have become the norm. In Proverbs 3:21 we are told to have two goals: wisdom and common sense. These will keep us from going astray and falling off the path; they will protect us. To counteract the worldly values taught in public schools and through secular media, we must teach our children to be wise and have discernment. We can provide them with a specific process for making good decisions, as opposed to the values clarification process for making decisions from a worldly point of view.

We can use values clarification games as a learning lab on how not to do it, then teach our children good decision-making skills. In fact, Citizens for Excellence in Education has published a book called *Escape From Sugarloaf Mine*, in which three popular values clarification exercises (the lifeboat game, nuclear fallout shelter, and cave-in) are woven together with three Bible stories to offer biblical solutions to these difficult moral dilemmas. This masterfully written book is geared to school-age children, with family application lessons perfectly suitable for use during Family Night. Our family has really enjoyed using them, and we all learned a lot! You can order *Escape From Sugarloaf Mine* by contacting CEE at the address/phone number at the back of this book.

Scriptural principles and Bible stories provide all the necessary wisdom for good decision-making. As parents, we can help our children by going with them to explore the Bible for solutions to the difficult questions they encounter. They will develop discernment as they learn to compare worldly advice to the Bible to see if that advice is correct.

> O Lord, the earth is full of your lovingkindness! Teach me your good paths. Lord, I am overflowing with your blessings, just as you promised. Now teach me good judgement as well as knowledge. For your laws are my guide.
>
> (Ps. 119:64-66, TLB)

> Your words are a flashlight to light the path ahead of me, and keep me from stumbling.
>
> (Ps. 119:105, TLB)

## WORLDLY DECISION-MAKING

A popular trend in education today is the teaching of "decision-making skills." Well, we'd all like for our children to know how to make decisions, wouldn't we? Unfortunately, the process that is generally used, values clarification, is antithetical to godly decision-making. If our kids follow the instruction of the public schools, they're likely to end up making some really poor decisions.

Remember: teaching children to make decisions is not the same as teaching them to make *good* decisions.

The schools may teach them to make decisions. But as Christian parents it is our responsibility to train our children to make *good, godly* decisions. Such conclusions can be based only upon a solid foundation of moral absolutes. Since the Bible is not allowed in public schools, and even the Ten Commandments are now denigrated as a religious violation of the separation of church and state, it is extremely difficult for public schools to teach good decision-making. They offer no guideline of moral absolutes against which students can judge actions.

Christian teachers try their best to bring moral principles into the schools, and certainly some curricula are better than others. But ultimately the responsibility for teaching good decision-making lies in the home, within the context of Christian values.

• A key flaw in worldly decision-making is its focus.

As Christian parents, we are educating our children for the *real* world—for eternity. But society teaches them that this earth is home, that this world is all there is. Worldly decision-making is focused on the present, not the future—on how to make the most of life on this earth. Children are torn between what we teach them at home and what society teaches.

• Worldly values conflict with Christian values.

Humanistic values are the norm in society and in public school curriculum. In fact, John Dewey, "the father of progressive education," was a major writer and signer of *Humanist Manifesto I* in 1933. Humanistic values teach our children:

"No deity will save us; we must save ourselves."
"Promises of immortal salvation or fear of eternal damnation are both illusory and harmful."

"Ethics [are] autonomous [individual] and situational, needing no theological or ideological sanction."

Humanism is selling our children a lie, telling them there is no God, there is no hope of salvation nor consequences of sin, and they must make up their own standards of right and wrong based on their own feelings in each situation.

• Worldly decision-making is based on moral relativism.

Children are taught that there is no right or wrong—all values are relative rather than absolute. Values clarification uses situation ethics, whereby the child makes up his own values, his own determination of what is right *for him at that particular time*, based on the situation and his own feelings.

## CLARIFYING VALUES CLARIFICATION

When your children are taught decision-making by values clarification or situation ethics, they are taught in this manner:

• *All* options must be considered in a situation.
• *Everyone's* idea of right and wrong is *equally valid*—it's just a matter of *personal opinion*.

Thus children are placed in a moral dilemma where they are forced to choose between *two wrong decisions* rather than a right one. For example, in the well-known lifeboat game, children must decide which four of ten passengers must die, since there is only enough food and water for six to live. Each passenger is described (i.e., an elderly man, a priest, a homosexual, etc.). The child is not allowed to refuse sentencing four to death, nor to offer himself in their place.

According to the values clarification process, based on Kohlberg's theories, all decisions must be made by adhering to the following steps. The decision must be:

1. Freely chosen.
2. Chosen from alternatives.
3. Chosen after careful consideration of the consequences.
4. Prized and cherished.
5. Publicly affirmed.
6. Acted upon.
7. Acted upon regularly.

It's interesting to notice that this is basically the same process the Bible teaches for a person who is becoming a new Christian. However, there are two fatal flaws:

- *God is absent* from the values clarification system.
- Helping children become good decision-makers will not necessarily help them make good decisions. When they freely choose to make a decision, they need to make it *within moral absolutes.* Both the Lord and parents can guide children to these biblical principles. Values clarification rejects such guidance and rejects the training children receive from their parents.

## NEUTRALIZING THE EFFECTS OF VALUES CLARIFICATION

Even if children are raised in an excellent Christian home, the teaching of situation ethics and value-free decision-making can be extremely detrimental. The values clarification technique is widely used in public schools and, sadly, even in some Christian schools.

When I was a senior in high school, I took a class called "Communications." The teacher drew much of her material from Sidney Simon's book *Values Clarification.* The class was worthwhile, and I learned a lot from it; but I had to participate in many "games" that forced me to make decisions that opposed my own Christian belief system. Thankfully, the teacher wasn't a situation ethics "purist" and actually contradicted many of Sidney Simon's ideas, neutralizing his influence somewhat.

Nevertheless, even with my solid Christian training, the values clarification exercises caused me some confusion and probably contributed to some poor decisions I've made. My parents were just becoming aware of the dangers of values clarification and tried to neutralize its effects as much as possible. I tell you this story simply to emphasize the important impact secular decision-making and problem-solving classes can have *even on Christian kids.*

Since values clarification techniques so subtly infuse many public-school courses, it is often impossible to withdraw your child from the class without actually sending him or her to a private school. Therefore, our focus will be on *neutralizing* the effects such teaching has on your child's life. You can do this through two avenues:

1. Changing what is taught in the classroom; and/or

2. Teaching your child God's moral standards and godly decision-making skills, so he or she can stand firm against false teaching.

To remove values clarification from the classroom, you will need to inform the teacher about your objections and the flaws in such teaching. In a nutshell, the problems with values clarification are:

- It is intrinsically hostile to tradition.
- It inherently opposes divine authority.
- Teaching only decision-making skills does not necessarily enhance moral development.
- When looking at the range of alternatives, family-held beliefs should be honored in all decision-making.

For a more detailed explanation of values clarification and its drawbacks, please write or call Citizens for Excellence in Education (see the back page of this book for the address/phone number) to ask for a free pamphlet on *Clarifying Values Clarification for the Innocent* by Education Research Analysts—Mel and Norma Gabler. You can give this pamphlet to your teacher. If the teacher is unsympathetic to your concerns, approach the principal, then the district superintendent, and finally your school board members. CEE can also recommend alternative curricula to teach values.

It is very difficult to teach values in the classroom since students come from such diverse cultural and religious backgrounds and each family's beliefs must be respected. Even many Christian teachers find themselves immersed in curricula that don't agree with their beliefs; but they've been taught to leave their Christian heart at the schoolhouse gate and work with a secular mind. These cases are sad because we desperately need good Christian teachers in the public schools who will stand firmly in their beliefs as role models for the children.

The second way to neutralize the effects of values clarification is to teach your child discernment. Situation ethics and the watering down of values is often taught very subtly. For instance, a teacher might raise the question, "Is it okay to steal?" Most Christian children would automatically respond, "No." The teacher would say, "In any situation?" Still, the response is, "No."

But what if the teacher then proposes a string of hypothetical moral dilemmas. "Would you steal food if your children were starving?" "If your mother was being unjustly imprisoned, would you steal the key to free her?" Using another example, that of lying, "Would you lie if you were hiding Jews in Nazi Germany?" "Would you lie to save your brother's life?"

These are difficult questions to answer, even for a mature Christian. Through such extreme cases the teacher builds a case for situations in which moral absolutes may appear not to hold true. Gradually, more situations are added until every situation requires a subjective moral decision to be made by the student. Children thus come to believe that they must decide when God's laws apply and when they do not, for their own life, at any given time. This opens the door to justification of any behavior, including sin.

You may not be aware that your child is subtly learning this humanistic philosophy in school. But you can become *proactively* involved, training your child in advance to make godly decisions and to recognize the false teaching of the world. You will neutralize the effects of such programs much better than you would with a negative reaction.

For instance, you can discuss the difficult moral dilemmas that I used as an illustration earlier. You can also discuss the alternatives to topics often found in public schools. For instance, when schools teach values clarification, you can talk about God's absolutes. When the topic of sex education arises, you can discuss the essentials of love and marriage. When abortion is promoted in schools, you can illustrate the value of a baby's life. When socialism is held up as an ideal, you can contrast it with the work ethic. And when evolution is taught, you can instruct your child about creation.

## MAKING GODLY DECISIONS

It's vitally important for children to learn to make *good, godly* decisions, not just how to make *a* decision. As Christians, every decision we make should be based on biblical values rather than on worldly ones. The Bible exhorts us:

> *Do not merely listen to the word, and so deceive yourselves. Do what it says.*
> (JAS. 1:22)

Teaching our children moral absolutes isn't enough to put them on auto-pilot. We must also train them in applying God's guidance to their everyday life in a practical way. We must teach them to apply their knowledge of the Word to making good decisions.

The following acrostic, using M-O-R-A-L-S, can be helpful in teaching our children a godly decision-making process. Notice the differences between this process and the one used in values clarification.

**M**     *Mindful of the Truth!* It's not enough to just know God's truth intellectually. Children must see its value and must learn to love the truth and want to obey.

**O**     *Observe Good Examples.* Children learn by *imitation*. Youth are challenged by *inspiration*. You can be an excellent model as a parent and also provide your child with suitable heroes.

**R**     *Read Virtuous Stories.* Expose your child to Bible stories, particularly those that teach principles they can apply practically to their own situation. Bible stories inspire and provide good role models.

**A**     *Assume a Moral Core.* Teach your children how things are, and uphold moral standards. This fixes limits and establishes order. Children don't need to ponder all the exceptions; that comes naturally.

**L**     *Look at the Options.* Not every option needs to be considered as an allowable option (e.g., homosexuality), but each must come under *biblical evaluation*, though only to the extent needed to determine if it is biblically acceptable.

**S**     *Standard Responses.* When your children are being pressured by their peers, you want them to have ready answers that they will speak without even thinking about it. They need to know standard responses to questions like:
- Is premarital sex wrong? Yes!
- Is honesty always right? Yes!
- Is stealing always wrong? Yes!
- Is it ever okay to use illegal or mind-altering drugs? No!

Practice decision-making with your child. Use examples from TV, books, or real-life friends to discuss what decision should have been made in a given situation. When our children come to us for advice, it's best to help them work through the decision on their own (they'll be more likely to stick by it), with our guidance through the M-O-R-A-L-S process.

You can even make a "what if?" game out of practicing good decision-making. For example, invent a fairly complex situation that is appropriate to the age and experience level of the child. Hand out "problems" on Monday. Then, during Family Night on Thursday (for example), let each child present his (or her) solution to the problem, including his reasons and scriptural principles to back up his reasoning. You might want to reward the effort in some small way if the answer and reasoning is sound. This will also reinforce a stock answer in the child, complete with reasons that will be retained since the child came up with them himself.

## HANDLING PEER PRESSURE

Peer pressure can have a positive or negative effect on a child, but often it's a negative one. Children are subjected to so many temptations at increasingly younger ages, including sex, drugs, drinking, violence, vandalism, and gangs. Gone are the days when gum chewing was a major classroom problem. Some of our children literally walk into a war zone every day when they go to school.

And we must not fool ourselves. These problems aren't limited to the inner city; they are common and prevalent in upper- and middle-class suburban and rural neighborhoods as well. Neither are such problems limited to public schools. I know many students at Christian high schools who tell me of the "double lives" their friends live. The parents think they have perfectly-trained, model Christian kids; but behind their backs their children are having sex and partying with their friends. No child is immune to peer pressure.

Our children will definitely be pressured to participate in some wrong activities (probably many). What's important is how they handle the pressure.

Training our children is the key! Teaching our children to have auto-pilot answers and make godly decisions is vitally important. However, sometimes teaching our children *to* say no isn't enough; we also need to train them *how* to say no.

First of all, you need to know what kinds of peer pressure your children are likely to be subjected to, then teach them specifically how to deal with those types of situations. Talk to them about how they *feel* and how they can have strength and confidence in their values and decisions, in addition to discussing how to deal with the situation at hand. Remember, most pressure plays on emotions and insecurities; so you'll want to arm your child against these tactics.

- *Very young children, under the age of six*, are most susceptible to manipulative threats by other children—for instance, being told that if they don't do something, no one else will like them or be their friends. Withdrawal of approval is used.

    Also, older children (or child abusers) may pressure younger children with the threat that they'll be punished or won't be loved or the parents will be injured if the child tells.

- *Elementary-age children* are most susceptible to pressure to conform or the desire to be in with the "in crowd." This stage will pass and usually only poses danger if the "in crowd" is involved in destructive behavior. Drugs may be introduced as early as elementary school. Children this age often have a fragile sense of confidence and are easily hurt and pressured by the group's taunts.

- *Pre-teens and teens* are most influenced by their best friends. Help your child make good choices in who to have as close friends. Discuss qualities that a true friend should have, and know your child's good friends and their families. Teens this age, trying to discover where they fit, experiment with hanging out with different crowds. Stay open and listen to your teen. Pay especially close attention when they say, "Everyone is doing it . . ." This could signal pressure to conform. Try to direct your child's search for individuality (even though it looks like conformity) into positive avenues such as leadership and Christian clubs.

At all ages and stages, children need guidance and strong standards more than they need space. As parents, it's our responsibility to listen and help; but we must always do this within a context of authority, where limitations and expectations are clearly established.

Here are some practical tips to teach your kids so they'll know *how* to say no:

- *Just say no and walk away*. Don't argue or discuss the issue any further. Show that you mean it.
- *Give reasons*. If a child is invited to a party where there will be drinking, he can tell his friends he already has other plans (if that is truly the case). Of if your daughter is offered drugs, she can say, "If I do drugs, I won't be able to win my track race, and that's more

important to me." Also, give your children permission to blame it on you: "My parents won't let me."

- *Suggest alternative ideas.* If a friend wants to engage in a negative behavior or the child is pressured for sex, he or she can suggest a different activity: "I know, let's go for ice cream instead." Or, "Let's go watch a video at my house." This rejects the activity, not the friend. It's especially wise to suggest a supervised setting.

- *Ask questions.* If the child has an uneasy feeling about a situation, he should ask more questions before entering into it. For instance: "Who will be there?" "Where is it?" "What will we do?" "Are there adults there?" "Can we get in trouble for this?" If the child has any doubts, he should refrain from the activity.

- *Ask permission.* A good way to get out of something with friends is for the child to say she has to ask her parents. Have a code word set up that means, "Say no." A code word you could use would be something like "Cool, Mom." When talking to Mom in front of a friend and the child *wants* mom to say no, she just includes in her request, "That would be cool, Mom." This helps the child save face with the friend without having to explain his or her uneasiness or the negative behavior to you in front of the friend.

- *Leave.* If the child feels threatened and his "no" answer or excuse is not being taken seriously, he should walk away and join another crowd of people, go home or to a class, etc.

Most importantly, try to keep the lines of communication open with your child. Let him (or her) know he can come to you *anytime* and tell you *anything*—that you are always there to help, listen, and offer unconditional love. But when you offer advice, remember to explain *why* you feel the way you do; offering examples from your own life is a powerful tool.

### Bringing It Home

*Applying God's Principles: Please refer to Chapter 2 for ideas on Family Night format and activities.*

Opening:     What are *morals*? How do they help us make good decisions?

Scripture:    Genesis 39:7-12 (Joseph's reaction to Potiphar's wife); Daniel 3 (the decision not to worship the golden idol); and 1 Samuel 24 (David's refusal to kill Saul).

**Discussion:**   Discuss the following questions after reading each Bible story:

1. What was the moral decision that had to be made?
2. Did the person make the *right* decision?
3. Upon which of God's principles was this decision based?
4. What was the result of this decision?

**Application:**   1. Review the M-O-R-A-L-S decision-making process. Ask the children if this differs from the way they are taught to make decisions or solve problems at school. If so, how?

2. Discuss a couple of hypothetical situations that your children could encounter (make them up based on what is appropriate for the ages of your children). Walk through the decision-making process together.

3. If you want to begin a weekly problem-solving game, you can start now.

# CHAPTER 15

◆

# *The Importance of Reading*

T he ability to read is essential to learning and is an important ingredient in a successful lifestyle. Since achieving all that God would have us do requires obeying Him, we must read His Word in order to ascertain His will and understand how we should live. As Christian parents, the ultimate goal in training our children is to enable them to successfully lead a godly life; this will require them to read and understand the Bible.

The Bible repeatedly instructs us to read it, for it is God's Word; it also emphasizes the value of reading.

*Blessed is the one who reads the words of this prophecy . . .*
(REV. 1:3)

*They read from the Book of the Law of God, making it clear and giving the meaning so that the people could understand what was being read.*
(NEH. 8:8).

Several issues come into play when we discuss the importance of reading. First of all, are your children able to read well? We're all aware of the shocking illiteracy rates among adults, which are a result of inadequate reading skills being developed while children are still in school. In fact, a nationwide study released by the U.S. Department of Education in 1993 reveals that *more than two-thirds* of America's fourth-, eighth-, and twelfth-graders *are not "proficient" readers!* A shocking statistic, to say the least, and one of which parents should be well-aware.

For our children to be fully successful in every area of their lives, they must be skilled readers. Only a small percentage of students at any grade level, between 2 and 4 percent, read at the "advanced level." This skill is vital to studying Scripture, succeeding in the workplace at any sort of skilled job, being safe, being a truly informed and discerning citizen, and having a high quality of life. Reading is important for learning, entertainment, and performing basic functions in society.

You can help your child become an outstanding reader. It's not difficult. This chapter will give you some tips.

Many schools are adopting a new learning approach called "whole language." With this method, children are taught to read by immersion in literature. Unfortunately, if whole language is not combined with intensive phonics, students learn only to "guess" at words, based on picture cues, context, and letter cues. (For more information on whole language, contact Citizens for Excellence in Education; the address and phone number are at the back of this book.)

If you don't feel your child is reading as he or she should, check to see what teaching methods are used in his or her school. Is *intensive* phonics incorporated? If it is not, you can teach your child at home using one of the many excellent phonics workbooks available at local bookstores or teacher-supply stores.

Even if our children *can* read, we must ask ourselves if they *do* read. Do our children read the Word and live their life by it, or do they model television personalities? A Gallup poll taken in the 1970s found that 82 percent of the elementary children polled *had not read a book* (any book) in the preceding month, but they had *watched nearly 100 hours of television!* I suspect the problem has increased rather than diminished since that time.

In addition to just making sure our children are *able* to read, parents play an important part in stimulating an *interest* in reading. A 1980 poll found that of 233,000 sixth-graders in California, only *three out of ten read for pleasure.* The other seventy percent are missing so much! I thank the Lord for parents that instilled in me, by example and inspiration, a love of the written word. Reading has brought me so much joy and relaxation—not to mention learning—throughout my lifetime!

The best way for parents to help their young children become better readers is to read to them. You can start reading to your child as soon as you start talking to him—at birth (some even do it during pregnancy!). And you should never stop.

There are many advantages to reading aloud to your child:

- It stimulates a child's *interest* in a subject.
- It aids in a child's *emotional development* (through the warm attention given by the parent).
- It stimulates a child's *imagination*.
- It improves a child's *language skills and vocabulary*.
- It *educates, entertains, explains, and inspires*.
- It causes a child to *enjoy books and learning*.

Reading to your child and helping him or her learn to read and understand the written word will give him or her great advantages in school, in life, and in serving the Lord.

The magnitude of importance placed on reading to small children is illustrated by Ruth Love, former superintendent of Chicago schools, who said:

> If we could get our parents to read to their pre-school children 15 minutes a day, we could revolutionize the schools.

When reading aloud, these tips are helpful to remember:

1. *Practice often.* Reading aloud is a skill that takes time to develop.
2. *Be expressive.* Read with emotion; make the material interesting.
3. *Adjust your pace* to fit the story. Slow down for suspense, speed up for a chase.
4. *Read slowly,* so the child has time to picture the scene.
5. *Have traditional reading times,* such as every evening after dinner or just before bed. If they wish, children can even play or draw while you read; this can help them use their imagination.
6. *Discuss the story.* Conversation is a vitally important part of reading. In helping develop the skill of reading comprehension, conversation also makes children realize that the purpose of reading is to gain information and insight, not just to decode words. Ask questions that require thinking and relate to everyday events. By asking questions beginning with the words who,

what, where, when, how, and why, you can help your child develop thinking skills.

7. *Don't use reading as a reward*; that could backfire on you if your children withhold their reading as a weapon. We want our children to *desire* to read.

8. *Fathers should read to their kids, too!* Most children are exposed to female teachers and see or hear their mother reading, but what about Dad? Fathers can help model the importance of reading.

9. *Listening must be learned*; it's not automatic. If your children are impatient or restless, let them play a little while you read; gradually they'll learn to listen quietly.

10. *Provide pencil and paper* to occupy those busy little fingers with writing or drawing.

11. *Model the importance of reading.* Your example speaks louder than words. Let your child see you reading. One way is to read a brief article aloud at the dinner table, then discuss it as a family.

12. *Love books.* Get excited about a book, and share your excitement with your kids. When I was young, one of my favorite books was *The Poky Little Puppy*. It was one of my mom's favorites when she was young, and she passed her excitement and love for the story on to me. Your excitement and love of books will rub off.

13. *Encourage reading just for fun*, as a free-time activity.

14. *Create an environment rich in books.* Take your children to the library so they can choose new books.

The U.S. Department of Education publishes a book called *Helping Your Child Learn to Read*; it offers more specific activities you can use with your child. The book is available through the *Consumer Information Catalog*, by writing to the Consumer Information Center, Pueblo, Colorado 81009.

In addition to reading to our children, we must give them opportunities to read to us and to read on their own. An older sibling may also enjoy reading to a younger sibling, or vice versa. Just fifteen minutes a day of silent reading, and another fifteen minutes a day of being read to, will make a tremendous difference in your child's life and his or her success at school.

When our children read to us, it is helpful to keep the following ideas in mind:

• *Phonics* are an integral part of reading. If your child has trouble sounding out the words, you can buy phonics workbooks for home use.

- While you don't want to discourage your child with negativity and correction, you can help him or her learn to *self-correct*. For example, if he reads a word incorrectly, help him to realize the sentence doesn't make sense or match the picture that way, then go back and help him sound out the words.
- *Patience* is the greatest challenge but is extremely important. Praise your child for his successful attempts.
- If the child is getting tired of trying, take over the reading for a few pages yourself, then *give her another chance.*

In addition to important reading such as Scripture and school texts, you can find many fiction and non-fiction books at your local Christian bookstore for your child's reading enjoyment and benefit. In addition to Bible storybooks and children's Bibles, these stores carry quality fiction reading that offers children inspiration and teaches valuable character lessons.

Personally, I like to screen *every* book, even those from Christian book stores, to make sure the story is age-appropriate and biblically sound. It's also especially important to review the literature your child reads at school.

### Bringing It Home

*Applying God's Principles: Please refer to Chapter 2 for ideas on Family Night format and activities.*

**Opening:**    Do you like to read? What kinds of books do you like to read and why?

**Scripture:**    2 Kings 22:8-20. You may wish to read from a children's version or to paraphrase the Scripture (or, better yet, explain the Scripture) for younger children.

**Discussion:**    What did Hilkiah the priest find? What did Shaphan do with God's Word? When he read it, what did he learn? As a result of that knowledge, what did the king do? What did God do when the king repented?

**Application:**   1. Why is reading valuable? (Example: for knowledge; for knowing God's will; for school and jobs;
for safety; for enjoyment.)

2. How does reading make you a better, more
discerning citizen?

3. Why is it important to read the Bible, in particular?

4. Each person in the family should choose something
they would like to read, then commit to reading for
ten or twenty minutes a day.

# CHAPTER 16

◆

# *The Art of Encouragement*

Perhaps one of the most important, and often most difficult, ways we can help our children succeed is to encourage them.

The very concept of encouragement can be daunting. What does it mean? How can I do it? Encouragement is one of those behaviors that's "easier said than done." The art of encouragement comes naturally to a few who are gifted; the rest of us have to develop our skill and work at this important, godly behavior.

Yes, I believe encouragement is a godly behavior. It is the act of *imparting courage* to another. By instilling courage in our children, we are building their confidence, helping them develop faith, and enabling them to deal with failure—three vital components of good parenting.

Our Heavenly Father is the perfect parent, and He exemplifies the art of encouragement. Which of us has not, at one desperate time or another, cried out in prayer and searched the Scriptures for encouragement? Did we not find it time and time again through our Lord's comforting words and the feeling of His love enveloping us? So many times it is exactly this heavenly encouragement that gives us the strength to go on; it lifts our wings and keeps us soaring.

My favorite passage of all time comes from Isaiah 40:29-31:

*He gives strength to the weary and increases the power of the weak. Even youths grow tired and weary, and young men stumble and fall; but those who hope in the Lord will renew their strength. They will soar on wings like eagles; they will run and not grow weary, they will walk and not be faint.*

I used to have this message printed on my key chain, and I'd turn to it many times throughout the day, just for a boost of encouragement. Of course I knew the words by heart, so all I had to do was look at my key ring and the passage would flood into my mind. I still cling to that verse whenever my human strength is failing me, which seems to be more and more frequently these days! With the Lord strengthening me, I can "soar on wings like eagles"! What an encouragement!

## ENCOURAGEMENT COMES FROM THE LORD

Our Heavenly Father is a God of encouragement. Romans 15:5, TLB says:

*May God who gives patience, steadiness, and encouragement help you to live in complete harmony with each other—each with the attitude of Christ toward the other.*

God encourages us and, in turn, intends for us to encourage others. Encouragement, like love, is meant to be shared. First Thessalonians 5:11 says: "Therefore encourage one another and build each other up."

Living a successful Christian lifestyle involves obeying God, as we have learned. Sometimes this obedience takes courage! But our God is our encourager. Read the story of Daniel, in Daniel 6. How would you like to face the challenges he endured? Daniel was a great man of God—truly a success. Certain men resented him for that reason, and they concocted a plan to try and force Daniel to disobey his God. Their plot was unsuccessful because Daniel knew that God would be faithful to him if he obeyed. And God delivered Daniel from the lions.

God will be faithful to us as well, if we obey. We can take courage in that fact. Our confidence, or courage, to obey comes from our knowledge of His Word. The Lord uses Scripture to encourage us; so we need to be strongly rooted in the Bible if we are to have courage ourselves and encourage our children. Daniel 11:32 (TLB) tells us that "the people who know their God shall be strong and do great things." Knowledge is a prerequisite for courage.

## SHARING YOUR COURAGE

Once we have received encouragement from the Lord, we're told to pass it on. Hebrews 3:13 exhorts:

*But encourage one another daily, as long as it is called Today . . .*

Encouragement should be part of our daily lives. And who better to practice it on than our family, with whom we interact each day? You can be a great blessing to your spouse and children simply by being an active encourager, like Barnabas was.

Barnabas, whose real name was Joseph, received his nickname because he was this type of person. "Barnabas" means "son of encouragement," a name that was aptly borne out in his life's ministry. He was a vitally important part of God's plan because he encouraged Paul and Mark in their ministries and encouraged many other believers as well. Think of what a great contribution he made simply by encouraging Paul, who in turn gave us so much wisdom through his Spirit-led writings! You've heard the saying, "Behind every good man is a great woman." Well, perhaps we should re-word that to read, "Behind every successful man or woman is an encourager."

Frequently encouragers receive no recognition, and their importance is seldom realized. But they *are* vitally important! You can have a wonderful ministry as an encourager to your family.

Barnabas had the courage to meet Paul after Paul was converted, even though Paul's reputation as a persecutor of Christians preceded him. Not only did Barnabas obey the Lord and meet Paul personally, but he also encouraged the other believers to trust Paul. He had courage himself, then shared it with others to support them and show them they could endure.

*When [Barnabas] arrived and saw the evidence of the grace of God, he was glad and encouraged them all to remain true to the Lord with all their hearts. He was a good man, full of the Holy Spirit and faith, and a great number of people were brought to the Lord.*
(ACTS 11:23-24)

*. . . strengthening the disciples and encouraging them to remain true to the faith.*
(ACTS 14:22)

Those words, written to describe Barnabas, are a testament to his successful lifestyle. I pray that similar words can someday be applied to each of us as we learn to receive encouragement from the Lord and pass it on to others, using it to build them into examples of godly success.

## OUR UNIQUE EQUIPMENT

You may be thinking, "I want to encourage my child. But exactly how do I encourage her? How do I do it?"

God has uniquely equipped each one of us to fulfill His purpose for our lives. Sometimes when we feel the Lord asking us to obey Him in a certain area we are tempted to say, "But, Lord, I just can't do that." I've made that mistake with my writing (as I'll share later); Moses made it with speaking. We've all felt that way at one time or another.

But God gives each of us different areas of skill, different strengths and abilities—different *specialties*, if you will. Our "equipment" wasn't assigned randomly. It was done according to God's purpose for each of our own lives. I recently took a spiritual gifts inventory and was surprised at some of the results. Some of the gifts indicated by the inventory didn't coincide with my own ideas of my strengths. However, after much thought and prayer, I could clearly see how I've actually had these gifts since I was a small child, and how God has developed and used them in ways that didn't readily come to my mind because I had not considered them significant. God often has a totally different perspective of our lives than we do. Exodus 28:3 shows God's specialization of his people:

> *"Tell all the skilled men to whom I have given wisdom in such matters that they are to make garments for Aaron, for his consecration, so that he may serve me as priest."*

In this example, God had given certain men technical skill to use in support of their leader, Aaron. Not all equipment leads to "glory jobs." But every job is important, and all of our unique equipment must be used properly if we are to be successful.

In Ezekiel 28:4-5 we see how the King of Tyre used his commercial skill wrongly—not in obedience to the Lord, for God's purposes, but rather for his own gain. This misuse of his unique equipment caused his downfall:

*"By your wisdom and understanding you have gained wealth for your-self and amassed gold and silver in your treasuries. By your great skill in trading you have increased your wealth, and because of your wealth your heart has grown proud."*

Each of us is entrusted with special gifts and abilities that are to be used in obedience and respected as special gifts from God. Paul explains it best:

*Yes, the body has many parts, not just one part. If the foot says, "I am not a part of the body because I am not a hand," that does not make it any less a part of the body. And what would you think if you heard an ear say, "I am not part of the body because I am only an ear, and not an eye"? Would that make it any less a part of the body? Suppose the whole body were an eye—then how would you hear? Or if your whole body were just one big ear, how could you smell anything? But that isn't the way God has made us. He has made many parts for our bodies and has put each part just where he wants it. What a strange thing a body would be if it had only one part! So he has made many parts, but still there is only one body.*

*The eye can never say to the hand, "I don't need you." The head can't say to the feet, "I don't need you."*

*And some of the parts that seem weakest and least important are really the most necessary.*

(1 COR. 12:14-22, TLB)

No matter how insignificant we believe our unique "equipment" to be, it is important, because God made us that way for a purpose. Each of us has a responsibility to the Lord to use our skills and talents for His glory, to fulfill His purpose for our life, as a member of our own family, our church, and the Church of God as a whole. We are part of each of these bodies.

It's important to teach our children and to recognize ourselves that we don't just *go to church.* As true believers in the Lord Jesus Christ we *are* the church. We should be reflecting a Christian lifestyle every day, no matter where we are, for we are representatives of Jesus. We have a duty to fulfill the role we've been assigned, using our unique skills and talents.

All we need to do is obey and become Christlike. We don't need to wait for more abilities to enable us to do it. We *can* do whatever God tells us to, by His power.

> *His divine power has given us everything we need for life and godliness through our knowledge of him who called us by his own glory and goodness.*
>
> (2 PET. 1:3)

When we were saved, God equipped us with everything we need for life and for serving Him, through the knowledge we gain in following Jesus and studying the Word of God. It's up to us to accept the opportunity and obey.

## HOW TO ENCOURAGE YOUR CHILD

According to Will Smith, star of TV's *The Fresh Prince of Bel-Air*, everything his father did, he did for a reason. So reported *Reader's Digest* in June 1993 (quoting Gail Buchalter in *Parade*). Smith recalls:

> Once Dad wanted my brother Harry and me to repair a 16-by-14 foot wall in front of his business. We had to dig a six-foot-long trench and rebuild the structure. It took six months.
>
> Years later Dad explained why he'd given us that task. "When a kid's growing up," he said, "he needs to see something that looks impossible to do, and then go out and do it. There are always going to be walls in life." My father helped us get over one wall, so we would never be scared to take the first step and try to do the impossible.

As parents we want to encourage our children to be godly successes and fully develop their unique God-given capabilities. How can we do this in a practical sense? There are several ways. First, we must understand several important distinctions.

• Obstacles can be viewed as possibilities.

Before we can help our children develop this mind-set, we must adopt it ourselves, which isn't always easy. I must admit, my first reaction to a challenge is avoidance and fear of failure. My husband, on the other hand, sees possibilities in everything and a way around any challenge.

We have some really neat items in our house because my husband saw potential in a piece of junk. In fact, the house we now live in was a real decorating challenge and required a lot of loving care and the ability to see potential. But God blessed us with a wonderful home, and through my husband's example I was able to see its potential and jump at the opportunity, rather than seeing its problems as too great an obstacle. Seeing around obstacles and challenges is one of the best skills I am developing. It enables me to take advantage of so many opportunities I otherwise would miss. Because I am learning these lessons myself, I will be able to encourage this positive mind-set in my children when they are tempted to shy away from a challenge for fear of failure.

Zig Ziglar once said, "A life freed from all obstacles and difficulties would reduce all possibilities and powers to zero." In fact, often when you take away the obstacle, you take away the ability. A motorboat's obstacle to going faster is the very same water it needs for propulsion. The obstacle that an airplane needs to overcome in order to fly faster is the very air it needs to keep flying.

The obstacles in our lives are necessary; they challenge us to succeed. As Chuck Swindoll once said, "We are faced with great opportunities brilliantly disguised as impossible situations."

• There is a fine line between encouragement and pressure.

Remember, encouragement means "instilling courage." If I tell my son, "You played a great game of soccer. Practice some more at making goals once you get near the goal—that's the only way you'll win," what is my message? That only "winning" is good enough.

When he does his best and brings home a B+ on his report card, am I encouraging him by saying, "That B+ is really good, and I'm proud of you. Next time I'd like to see an A"? Notice that I've been careful to avoid negating my statement with a "But," but nevertheless I have used my praise to pressure my son.

Encouragement should be like God's love—unconditional. By instilling courage, we simply want to build the child up to be a success, not pressure him or her to do more or do better. We can make our encouragement unconditional by focusing on positive actions, positive potentials, and even positive aspects of failure (which we'll talk about later).

• Praise and encouragement are *both* necessary.

We often think of praise and encouragement as the same thing, since praise also has the effect of encouraging us. But they are distinctly different. *Praise* focuses on the act, the actual achievement that takes place. Thus praise usually comes as the result of success. If you have a good sales record for the month, your boss will praise you. If your child gets an A in math, you praise him or her.

*Encouragement*, on the other hand, focuses on effort. It can take place throughout the process of trying, anywhere along the path of life. For example, your boss encourages you by saying, "You're really being diligent about those calls—I know it will pay off for you." You can encourage your daughter by saying, "I saw how you shared your doll with Susie. That showed how generous you are. Doesn't that make you feel good? God likes it when we're friends with people and are generous and share."

Encouragement builds feelings of adequacy. Simple statements such as "I like the way you handled that," "I know you can do it," or "You're improving" can boost the child's confidence and encourage more of that behavior in the future. It's even more encouraging if you can affirm a specific character quality in your child. If you say, "You're improving," add, "You really have a good eye for detail." Encouragement can come in the form of a spoken word, a note in the lunch box, listening and nodding, or even a special hug.

Here are some tips to help you distinguish and focus on encouragement, going beyond praise:

1. Identify what the child did.
2. Comment on the character quality that was reflected (i.e., honesty, kindness, cleanliness, diligence, etc.).
3. Make a positive statement/belief about their future (i.e., "I believe your diligence will make you a great success in the future").

Like encouragement, praise will be most effective if it focuses on a specific action and emphasizes an inner quality. When I say, "Thanks for helping me with the dishes. You really are a hard worker," I am encouraging as well as praising by focusing on a positive character quality. The child can also see that I am sincere.

• Labeling children is the opposite of affirming them.

Affirmation of our children, for their internal character qualities and also for their actions, is vitally important. Affirmation can be given through praise or encouragement.

A lack of praise may cause the child to continually seek praise through ways of obtaining worldly success. The child may believe (based on what society clearly implies is "good enough") that money, fame, and other symbols of success will lead to his or her parent finally saying, "You've done well. I am proud of you. I love you."

A constant diet of praise (genuine and well-deserved), and especially encouragement, will make children feel loved and accepted for who they are, not simply for what they achieve.

A child's self-concept, how he perceives himself, should be based on *who he is* (who God created him to be) rather than how well he performs. Reinforcing your child's good internal qualities will help him develop an accurate self-concept based on his Creator rather than on his achievement.

Labeling our children is the opposite of affirming them. Labeling can have a profound effect, even when done innocently, without bad intentions. A child, like any of us, remembers negative comments much more readily than positive ones. One negative outweighs ten positives. Even a comment not intended by the parent to be negative and not stated in a negative tone can convince the child, over a period of time, that it is true. A friend of mine found this to be so, for example, by calling her son "our little brat." Even though it was meant teasingly and lovingly, such a repetitive label could convince the child it is true. She certainly didn't want the child to *become* a brat!

Obviously, not every interaction we have with our children will be positive and affirming. Children do disobey, and they need to be corrected. However, it is possible to focus correction on the behavior without casting negativity on the child. For instance, I could say, "Taking that toy away from your brother was not very nice. We don't play that way. I know you want to be generous, so let's share next time." Keep the negativity focused on the wrong behavior, not on the child (i.e., "You are very selfish"); then encourage the behavior you'd like to see in the future.

When criticism is necessary, we can even encourage our children within that context by making our comments constructive and framing them in uplifting words. First, tell your child what he or she is doing right. Then discuss what he or she is doing wrong and *why* it is wrong. Close with a plan for doing better, emphasizing the character traits your child has that will help him or her to eliminate the wrong behavior and change it to good.

Charles Schwab said, "I have yet to find a man—however exalted his position—who did not do better work and put forth greater effort under a spirit of approval than under a spirit of criticism." The Bible, too, warns us of the dangers of discouragement.

*Fathers, don't scold your children so much that they become discouraged and quit trying.*

(COL. 3:21, TLB)

## HELPING YOUR CHILD REACH HIS POTENTIAL

Earlier we discussed our own definition of "potential"—*helping our children make the most of their abilities*. Realistically, potential is not a point of success children attain; it is a process of living a successful, godly lifestyle to the best of their ability. As parents, we all want to help our children achieve their "potential"—academically, morally, and spiritually. But we also realize that many children are unsuccessful in doing so. What can you as a parent do to help your child maximize his or her abilities?

First of all, you must help your child to realize that he or she *has* potential. No child is doomed to failure; all have the ability to achieve to some degree. Every one of us can live successfully. As a parent, you'll want to have realistic expectations and awareness of your child's strengths and weaknesses, so you can help guide him toward positive experiences without pressuring him.

While some children are naturally motivated and confident, many children must be *guided* to the realization that they are *capable* of achieving. Underachievers have more ability than they are using; but with proper motivation and increased awareness of their abilities, they will gain confidence and success. Overachieving children, on the other hand, may achieve way beyond their ability level, which could cause problems if their life becomes unbalanced (i.e., if they are too "driven" by their academic or sports achievement, to the neglect of their spiritual and family life).

The key for parents is to *guide* their children. Guidance differs from pressure (which is a negative motivation) and from artificially contrived achievement experiences (in which the child may feel deceived or feel that the "set-up" was necessary because he lacks ability).

Orchestrating success, or guiding a child to achieve, means creating an environment in which your child can truly succeed.

A child acquires confidence in his own abilities a little bit at a time as he tries them out and experiences a feeling of success. Achievement rarely happens by accident, though. Achievers set goals for themselves and have a plan of action to reach those goals. If a child has no goals, he will have no action, and he will lack accountability to himself.

The attainment of a goal, however small, provides an opportunity for a child to acquire an inner sense of satisfaction and self-confidence, which will help him reach his potential by making full use of the abilities God has given him.

As parents, we should look for the best way possible to be *encouragers* as we guide our child to achieve. How can you do this in a practical way? First, identify one area in which your child shows interest. For example, perhaps your ten-year-old daughter is interested in cooking.

Second, help your child set a goal that will help her develop that area of interest. In this example, the goal may be to cook an entire Sunday dinner for the family.

Next, help your child decide on a plan of action—steps she must take to achieve her goal. Remember, you are there to *guide*, not to do it for her. She will gain a sense of accomplishment only if she is "in charge" of the decision-making. In this example, a possible plan of action is:

*Step 1*: Decide on a menu.
*Step 2*: Shop for ingredients.
*Step 3*: Follow recipes carefully.
*Step 4*: Serve the meal creatively.

When praising your child, focus on the inner qualities that were exhibited by the action, not just the activity itself. This will help the child realize her potential in relation to character traits, not just have one successful experience. In this example, you could affirm your daughter for her imagination, for being organized and conscientious, for being artistic and creative, and for paying attention to detail. It's often easier to focus on our children's negative qualities and behaviors, since they really get under our skin, than to comment on their positive attributes. Each child has positive inner qualities that we can begin to encourage and emphasize. Such qualities may include:

| | | | |
|---|---|---|---|
| Artistic | Caring | Committed | Compassionate |
| Confident | Conscientious | Considerate | Courageous |
| Dependable | Encouraging | Energetic | Enthusiastic |
| Fair | Friendly | Generous | Gentle |
| Goal-oriented | Good listener | Hard worker | Honest |
| Humorous | Imaginative | Intelligent | Knowledgeable |

| Loving | Loyal | Mechanical | Neat |
| Obedient | Optimistic | Organized | Persistent |
| Personable | Positive | Possesses faith | Resilient |
| Responsible | Thoughtful | Understanding | Wise |

An easy way to identify which of these traits your child already possesses is to observe his or her behavior (or to remember past behaviors) and identify which characteristic the action involved. For example, if your child worked three hours on homework, this demonstrates traits of being responsible and conscientious.

Now that your child has successfully reached a goal in one area of interest, repeat your guiding, or orchestrating, for achievement in other areas, like academic, spiritual, vocational, social, civic, or physical.

Imagine a rope. Each *cord* of the rope is comprised of many *threads*. Let each thread represent an inner quality. Many threads (inner qualities) make us successful in an area of life, which is represented by a cord. *Cords* (which could represent different areas of life—i.e., academic, spiritual, social, etc.) make up a *rope*, representing a complete and balanced life that will result as your child achieves his potential in individual threads.

Each success has a spill-over effect into other areas, since you are affirming the child's core qualities, not just outside activities. Qualities shown by the meal planning, like attention to detail or being organized and conscientious, will also be important factors in achieving success in other areas, like academics.

## How Expectations Affect Your Child

*For as he thinketh in his heart, so is he.*
(PROV. 23:7, KJV)

One of the most powerful forces in human relationships is expectation. Expectations can be powerful or devastating. Think about it: you pattern your life around expectations—from God, your church, your spouse, your family, your children, your employer, your country, your friends, yourself.

We are each expected to live a certain way, to believe a certain way, to think a certain way, and to act a certain way. These expectations drive us toward our achievements. In fact, they determine many of our actions. Some of our most important choices are based on others' expectations.

The same is true of our children.

If I believe my child will disappoint me or fail to perform, he will probably "live down to" my expectation. On the other hand, children will also rise to (live up to) our expectations if we believe they have the ability to achieve and if we encourage them along the way.

• Expectations can help a child gain confidence.

Your child will be more successful in achieving her desired objective if she believes in her ability to do so. You can give her confidence through your positive expectations and your praise of her abilities and good character traits. Your encouragement will help breed confidence.

If you want to raise your children to achieve great things, you need to frequently assure them that they are winners—that they have the ability to achieve. Let them know that God has equipped them with every talent and ability they need to serve Him and to live a successful Christian lifestyle in each facet of their lives—and that He will give them the strength to do so.

We all strive for significance. You can imagine how much your acknowledgment and affirmation mean to your children. They love you most and want you to be proud of them. I think one of the most common mistakes we make as parents is not our lack of pride in our children, but rather our failure to communicate that pride. When you feel proud of your son, tell him. When your daughter shows a great character quality, tell her how proud it makes you to see her acting in such a godly manner.

Children don't need constant reminders of their inadequacies or of their own smallness. They are well aware of those!

• Expectations set moral standards in a family.

If you communicate clear expectations to your children in areas of temptation, they will be more likely to make godly choices. Train your children in God's (and your own) expectations that they will remain pure, will not take drugs, and will be honest and live righteous lives. If your expectations are clear in these areas, and they understand God's instruction, their actions and choices will be affected.

• Affirmation must be meaningful to be effective.

Believing that good self-esteem will help a child achieve academically, many public schools have gone too far, positively reinforcing substandard work (i.e., not correcting spelling or not assigning any grade below a C) for fear of damaging the child's self-esteem. As well-intentioned parents, we can easily fall into the same trap.

The truth is that a child's confidence in his abilities comes from repeated success and achievement, not the other way around. Studies bear this out. Certain standards must be upheld, or teachers and parents are not doing the students any favor.

Help your child build confidence through encouragement and genuine affirmation, not through empty praise. If we praise every tiny, inconsequential thing they do, our affirmation becomes meaningless. Children can tell if our words come from our heart.

• Expectations must be realistic.

Just as the theory of positive expectation should not be used to reward failure, neither should it be used to "puff up" a child's ego or set unrealistically high expectations that result in failure. In Romans 12:3 Paul tells us:

> For by the grace given me I say to every one of you: Do not think of yourself more highly than you ought, but rather think of yourself with sober judgment, in accordance with the measure of faith God has given you.

For a child to be successful in God's eyes, he or she must be obedient and live in His will. As parents, we can focus on the child's ability to do this (the positive), while still training the child in humility. Humility does not mean having a negative view of oneself, just a realistic understanding of our relationship to God.

This verse also communicates the idea that God has given each of us certain talents, abilities, and limitations. We must recognize these and do our best *within* that realm. Obviously, we have many genetic, physical limitations as well as gifts. We have certain spiritual strengths as well on which we should focus.

You can help your child understand God's will for his or her life, set realistic goals to achieve it based on his or her own unique strengths and weaknesses, and affirm the abilities that God has created within him or her to enable him or her to accomplish what He asks. This will help her to achieve godly success.

• Parental models create powerful expectations.

Earlier we discussed the powerful influence your own lifestyle has on your child's development. Each of us creates certain expectations within our family in very subtle ways, simply by the way our family operates. These can be positive or negative.

For instance, when you were first married you were probably keenly aware of the impact your own parents' habits and behaviors had on you. What we observe in our own homes generally becomes our perception of "normal." When I was growing up, I was fortunate to have a mother who stayed home and had plenty of time for us. She had cookies and milk ready when I arrived home from kindergarten; she would sit and play games or cards or blocks with us for hours. She kept the house immaculate and sewed many of my clothes. She always had a well-balanced meal on the table when my dad got home from work. I had a "supermom" who did everything.

My husband, on the other hand, came from a background where he observed his mother work hard each day. She left the house before he left for school. His wonderful model of a father made breakfast and a sack lunch for his wife. Dinner and housework were shared duties, and the family didn't always eat together. While my husband had a wonderful family, it was very different from my own.

We each came into marriage with different role expectations, based on our parental models. Although I worked, I felt I must be superwoman. I spent all my free evening and weekend time cleaning and cooking, trying to create what I perceived to be the perfect home for my husband. Because we have excellent communication, I soon found out that he felt neglected; he thought his wife should be free to spend time with him and not be so focused on the house.

It was very hard for me to let go of my own expectations of myself and not feel the house had to be perfect. I had to realize that the circumstances of my life were not the same as my mother's; nor were my husband's expectations of me the same as mine for myself. Throughout our marriage I have come to accept some help with cooking (Tim enjoys it!), cleaning, and even home decorating.

An example of a negative modeling expectation would be a home where the parents deal with problems by arguing. A child who grows up with this sees it as a normal, viable way to deal with controversy. It will become that adult child's automatic response. (Or he might turn away from the pattern in such dramatic ways that an entirely different set of problems is created, such as an unwillingness to communicate or to talk things out. Neither of these extremes is preferable, godly, or healthy.)

As parents, we need to be aware of the subtle expectations we create in our home and discuss them with our children. Exposing our kids to other families' way of doing things (i.e., dividing chores) and presenting it simply as a different way, not a "bad way," will help our children adjust to the needs of their future spouse.

## *Bringing It Home*

*Applying God's Principles: Please refer to Chapter 2 for ideas on Family Night format and activities.*

**Opening:** What does it mean to *encourage* someone? Why is encouragement important?

**Scripture:** 1 Corinthians 12:14-22. (*The Living Bible* is easy for children to understand.)

**Discussion:** What special functions do various parts of our human bodies have, like the eye, the ear, the stomach, the foot? Does each person in a family contribute to the whole family in a special way? How? Do various people at church contribute in unique ways to the whole church (i.e., the pastor, a teacher, a greeter, a singer)?

**Application:** 1. Have each person in the family write down one special quality or ability that each of the other family members contributes to your home. If jobs are listed, try to think of a character quality exhibited in that activity. Share aloud with each other.

2. Why is it important to encourage each other to use the talents and abilities God has given you all? How can God use you to encourage others?

3. Each person should list one specific way in which he or she will encourage each of the other family members this week. Also determine one way to encourage a a friend this week.

# CHAPTER 17

◆

# *Helping Your Child Handle Failure*

Thomas Edison was mocked for trying, unsuccessfully, some 5,000 materials for the filament of his great dream, the incandescent light-bulb. "You failed 5,000 times," said a critic of his day. "I have not failed," countered Edison, "I have discovered 5,000 materials that won't work."

Thomas Edison knew how to handle what others perceived to be failure. I imagine you'd have to be pretty good at seeing obstacles as opportunities to be a scientist or researcher, wouldn't you? But if there were no people of great vision, like Thomas Edison who kept on trying after many apparent failures, we would lack the necessary medical technologies and conveniences we have today.

The lesson of Thomas Edison teaches us that failure moves us closer to success—if we learn from our mistakes and keep trying! Achievement takes work!

Zig Ziglar says it well:

Knowing how to benefit from failure is the key to success.

Some of the most difficult times for a parent to endure and handle are those times when they must watch their child fail. To see those downcast eyes and dejected shoulders is almost physically painful to a parent. Oh, that we could bear such burdens for them!

It's so tempting, and natural, for us to desire to protect our children from failure. If only they could be successful in everything they attempt! But would that really benefit the child? We want our children to grow and mature, and failure is a vitally important part of that process, as painful as it may be. Certainly we don't need to orchestrate failure to help our children grow; they will encounter plenty of difficulties on their own as they journey down the path of life.

Romans 5:3 (TLB) tells us the purpose of failure:

*We can rejoice, too, when we run into problems and trials, for we know that they are good for us—they help us learn to be patient.*

The passage goes on to say:

*And patience develops strength of character in us and helps us trust God more each time we use it until finally our hope and faith are strong and steady.*
(ROM. 5:4, TLB)

Isn't that our goal for our children? That they develop inner character, learn to trust God, and develop a hope and faith that are strong and steady? I'm sorry, but Paul says that failure, difficulties, and trials make up the first step in this growth process. I wish it weren't so, but looking back on my own life, I can see how very true those words are.

We all want to protect our children from difficulty, hurt, and disappointment. But sometimes these "negatives" are necessary prerequisites for the positives to occur. Keeping our children from pursuing a goal that they may not be able to reach, in an effort to protect them from failure, may not be doing them a favor.

*Tough times develop character, and character is what gets us through those tough times.*

Interestingly enough, avoiding failure is one of my own greatest character flaws. Despite my parents' encouragement while I was growing up, I never tried out to be a cheerleader because I was afraid I wouldn't make it. I never ran for a school office because I was afraid I wasn't good enough. I even left the NACE/CEE ministry for a while rather than try my hand as a writer because I was afraid I would fail.

Oh, sure, I never *said* I was afraid to fail. I always had a list of logical reasons why the timing was bad, it was too expensive, etc. But deep down inside I wanted to try for these things and didn't because I was afraid.

Ironically, my little sister, Mandi, tries everything. She never fears failure. I have seen her very upset because she ran for class president (I think it was in the fifth grade) and didn't make it. But she bounced back from failure and kept trying other things. She plays three varsity sports and competes in equestrian hunting and jumping events. I never tried out for a team, afraid I wouldn't make it.

Did Mandi's failures, even at a very young age, hurt her confidence? No. Somehow they built it.

She has the confidence to accept challenges rather than take the easy road. As a thirteen-year-old, Mandi gave up riding a championship horse, on which she could win a blue ribbon in almost every competition, to accept the challenge of training an older, untrained range pony. With perseverance and a lot of hard work, she was able to take this pony to the championship show within eight months. Facing challenges head-on has helped Mandi develop a wonderful, strong character full of hope and faith.

Did my own avoidance of failure give me confidence? (I can truly say I've never really failed—at anything I've *tried*, that is.) No. In fact, perhaps I feel like more of a failure for never trying in the first place. I still struggle with confidence to this day! But now I forge ahead and try new things, because God has given me the courage to overcome my own fears. I cling to the verse:

> *And he said unto me, My grace is sufficient for thee: for my strength is made perfect in weakness. Most gladly therefore will I rather glory in my infirmities, that the power of Christ may rest upon me.*
> (2 COR. 12:9, KJV)

Our weaknesses and failures are the perfect opportunities for Christ's strength to shine through us, for His power to rest upon us. What an enabling truth! We need not be afraid.

Teddy Roosevelt had it right when he said:

> The credit belongs to the man who is actually in the arena; whose face is marred with dust and sweat; who strives valiantly; who falls and may fall again and again, because there is no effort without error or short-comings.

I've often thought, "Why does God lead us to pursue a certain direction that leads to failure?" God doesn't take all the difficulty out of our lives. In fact, sometimes He leads us right into it. That's because God is a loving parent who wants us to grow, and He knows that trying and failing, and trying again and again, leads us through that process of spiritual growth and character development. Through this natural process we become who God intends for us to be.

The same is true with our children. Their character grows through adversity. If they are overprotected, they become overdependent and weak and can't act on their own.

So, what is the lesson for parents in following our Heavenly Father's example?

- *We should allow our children to fail.* If we hinder this process, we are hindering their growth.
- *Remind the child that failing doesn't make him or her a failure.* Everyone fails at some attempts.
- *We should always be there to "pick up the pieces," to encourage our children through their failure.* We can do this by relating Thomas Edison's story or Teddy Roosevelt's quotation. Show your child how people he knows who are a great success have experienced many failures. Focus on the positive learning experience that occurs through such situations.
- *Help your child develop hope and faith through failure.* Share God's assurances with him or her.

> *A righteous man may have many troubles, but the Lord delivers him from them all; he protects all his bones, not one of them will be broken.*
> (Ps. 34:19-20).

No one can take away our eternal life, even if they kill us!

> *"Happy are those who are persecuted because they are good, for the Kingdom of Heaven is theirs."*
> (Matt. 5:10, TLB)

- *Help your child see the failure as an obstacle to overcome, a challenge.* Also, be realistic.
- *Resist the urge to blame the failure on someone else or on circumstances.* This teaches the child that it is unacceptable to fail. Allow the truth to stand; help the child get past it and go on to new achievements.

- *Help your child remember that usually the fun, the experience, and the learning come in the process of trying, not in the act of winning.* My husband's work as a physical therapist illustrates the important line we must walk in orchestrating our child's success and yet allowing him to handle failure. When Tim sees a patient in the hospital rehabilitation unit, he concentrates on orchestrating small, constant successes so the patient will develop hope and begin to feel confident that he will recover from his injury or debilitation.

However, by the time this same patient reaches Tim in the outpatient rehabilitation department, the patient is at a completely different stage in the healing process. The patient is learning to function again in the "real world" and must be allowed to fail at some things while succeeding at others. When the patient experiences failure in an attempt, he realizes the need to overcome the weakness and is motivated to try harder. Through the process of overcoming the obstacle, the patient develops real confidence in his ability to overcome future obstacles, rather than carrying an unrealistic expectation that he will only experience success.

So it is with children. They need to experience success, and parents can help them encounter situations where they are likely to succeed. While this will help them build some sense of confidence, true courage is built by overcoming obstacles—triumphing over failure. So we mustn't prevent them from experiencing those challenges.

## Overcoming Fear

Courage casts out fear. When we are fearful and therefore fail to obey the Lord, we miss out on many blessings. For example, God gave the Israelites the Promised Land, a land "flowing with milk and honey." Obviously, the people looked forward to this paradise after the slavery of Egypt. Nevertheless, they were terribly frightened by stories about giants that inhabited the land, and they lacked the courage to obey God and enter their paradise.

Rather than receiving courage from God, they let fear overcome them. They lacked faith. And they were sentenced to forty more years of wandering in the desert.

Why does the Bible contain such detailed descriptions of Jewish history? Why are even their failures carefully recorded? In large part, so that we will learn from the past.

*For everything that was written in the past was written to teach us, so that through endurance and the encouragement of the Scriptures we might have hope.*

(ROM. 15:4)

We are wise to learn from these examples and not make the same mistakes. God intends for the testimony of His glory and victory to encourage us to obey Him today and live successfully.

Many times we face situations that are intimidating or frightening. A physical threat, like the lions Daniel faced, can be terrorizing. But so can an emotional threat—like God asking us to do something that takes us out of our comfort zone. For some, this may be an experience like public speaking or teaching. For others, it may be parenting or reentering the workforce or even coping with the death of a close relative.

Moses faced such a dilemma when God appointed him to lead the Israelites:

*But Moses pleaded, "O Lord, I'm just not a good speaker. I never have been, and I'm not now, even after you have spoken to me, for I have a speech impediment."*

*"Who makes mouths?" Jehovah asked him. "Isn't it I, the Lord? Who makes a man so that he can speak or not speak, see or not see, hear or not hear? Now go ahead and do as I tell you, for I will help you to speak well, and I will tell you what to say."*

(EXOD. 4:10-12, TLB)

Like me, perhaps you feel you've had a similar discussion with the Lord. Writing was just such a challenge to me. I would constantly ask the Lord, "Why me? I can't write well enough. I'm just a nobody." And the Lord would say, "Obey Me."

After I had worked at Citizens for Excellence in Education for about six years, in many capacities, we brought on a new general manager. Since I had written some short radio scripts and a workbook, he decided I should do research and writing full-time. He was a godly man, trying to position all the staff members in order to utilize the gifts he felt God had given them.

I resisted this calling. In fact, I decided to leave the ministry for a while and "try my wings in the 'real' world." I did desktop publishing for an investment company for a few months before God called me back to CEE. I told the manager I would come back under one condition—no writing. I was too afraid of failure in that area. So I worked my way through some other new responsibilities, like setting up events and eventually management.

Finally, God called me so unmistakably and loudly to write that I had no choice. To my great surprise, He has greatly used the materials I've produced (with a lot of help from the Holy Spirit).

It amazes me to this day, and I still find myself so lacking in confidence in this ability that I must simply obey the Lord because He has called me to be a writer.

I don't particularly enjoy writing, and I certainly don't see it as my strength. I can think of many ways I would rather serve the Lord. But I have concluded, like Moses and Jonah, that God knows better than we do what needs to be done. And He calls us according to *His* plan, not our desires.

Our job as servants of the Most High is not to evaluate His requests. We are simply to *obey*.

God may be using us in an area where we think we are weak. Perhaps that ensures that our own ego does not get in the way; we are forced to depend upon the leading of His Holy Spirit (to be a *servant*). Also, stretching our comfort zone of service is one way in which God trains us and "grows" us. To fail to obey is to lose the opportunity to serve the Lord, and also to miss the opportunity for growth that He is offering to us.

By *fearing* failure we may *fail* to use the gifts God has given us, which we're told in 1 Timothy 4:14 not to neglect. Instead, we should step out in faith and act.

Whatever God asks us to do, He will enable us to do. He will give us the courage if we obey Him in faith.

*For God hath not given us the spirit of fear, but of power, and of love, and of a sound mind.*

(2 Tim. 1:7, KJV)

*"So do not fear, for I am with you; do not be dismayed, for I am your God. I will strengthen you and help you; I will uphold you with my righteous right hand."*

(Isa. 41:10)

*"For I am the Lord, your God, who takes hold of your right hand and says to you, Do not fear; I will help you."*

(Isa. 41:13)

Next time you feel afraid or are challenged to obey God by performing outside your comfort zone, imagine Him holding your right hand and giving you strength. Remember these verses of encouragement that God has given to you.

Our faith will give us courage. And the Lord will be faithful. In Matthew 9 a woman of great faith believed that if she could just touch Jesus' garment, she would be healed. She was not afraid, and Jesus did heal her, saying, "Daughter, be of good comfort; thy faith hath made thee whole . . ." (Matt. 9:22, KJV). We can always have courage through knowing that the Lord is in control of *everything*. Our courage comes from this faith in Jesus.

### Bringing It Home

*Applying God's Principles: Please refer to Chapter 2 for ideas on Family Night format and activities.*

**Opening:** What is failure? Give some examples of failure. Is failure good or bad? Should we avoid failure?

**Scripture:** Luke 22:54-62.

**Discussion:** Peter, one of Christ's closest friends, failed Jesus badly. How did he do this? How was this failure used to make Peter a great success? (How did remembering Christ's words affect his life? How great was his commitment to Christ later in his ministry?) When we fail and show our weakness, how can Christ use that? How is He our strength?

**Application:** 1. Have each person think of one thing in his or her life he or she considers to have been a failure. Share this with the rest of the family.

2. Together, have the family discuss how this "failure" was a learning experience to spur that person on to success. What did he or she learn from the experience? If the failure was very recent, you can discuss how the person can use this weakness to grow.

3. What character traits did the failure (or the process that resulted in failure) help develop? How can these be used in the future?

# CHAPTER 18

♦

# *Discipline: Beyond Punishment*

Whenever you hear the word *discipline*, what is the first meaning you think of? Many of us quickly conjure up images of being spanked, told to stand in the corner, or punished by withdrawal of favorite activities. In actual fact, the definition "treatment that corrects or punishes" is listed *fifth* out of five definitions given in the *New World Dictionary*, 2nd edition.

The word *discipline* comes from the Latin *discipulus*, from which we also get the world *disciple*. Now, what images does the word *disciple* bring to your mind? Jesus' twelve devoted followers, dedicated to modeling His ways and learning from Him? Quite a different perspective than the one we think of for our children, isn't it?

In this chapter we will touch on correction and punishment, but we will focus on discipleship. I like the dictionary definition that considers discipline to be "training that develops self-control, character, or orderliness and efficiency." Isn't that what we really strive for with our children, even through correction?

## DISCIPLING YOUR CHILDREN

As a parent, each of us holds a powerful position of great responsibility. God has entrusted us with His precious little ones, to help them develop into all He intends for them to be. Particularly when our children are little, they look up to us as though we are God. They watch our every action and hang upon our every word. They want to be just like Mommy and Daddy. It sounds a bit like the way Jesus' disciples, His babes in the Lord, looked up to Him. What a tremendous responsibility we have in training these little ones!

When the Lord gives us a task, He always gives us guidance in how He would like it performed. In the case of discipling our children, He has given us not only the model of Jesus and His disciples, but plenty of specific instruction directed at parents, throughout the Bible. We have covered much of this instruction through the course of this book. Discipleship really ties together all the principles that we've been learning, since it is the process of training our children.

Let's look at some key elements of Christ's training of His followers:

- He modeled godly behavior for them to follow.
- He instructed them in the ways of the Lord and used life as a classroom.
- He helped them gain a proper understanding of godly success as opposed to worldly success and called them to let go of their earthly treasures and follow Him, making their Christian walk top priority.
- He taught them to pray and made prayer and scriptural teaching part of their daily lives.
- He imparted wisdom and taught them God's will.
- He encouraged the disciples, allowed them to fail at times, and helped them learn from their weaknesses.
- He was perfectly consistent.

Sound familiar? These are the concepts we've been covering in this book—the key elements in training your children to be successful. I address discipline as a separate element, as part of the training process, because so many people equate discipline with punishment. But it really runs parallel to the training process and is closely related. Training and discipline are integral parts of one another.

To be effective trainers of our children, we must model Christ's training of His disciples.

## WHY DISCIPLINE?

We need to view discipline in two major categories. First, *there is the discipline that we impart to our children*. This discipline includes modeling and teaching. It also includes correction.

Second, *we must help our children develop self-discipline.* We all recognize that it's virtually impossible to *force* our children to behave the way we would like, to *force* them to be responsible and obedient. If that's your plan for making your child successful, I hate to be the bearer of bad news, but it ain't gonna work! It might seem like it's working for a while, but ultimately your child will reach adulthood and live exactly as he or she pleases.

Our goal is to train and equip our children so that they handle independence in a godly fashion—so they're on auto-pilot! We want to develop the holy character in our children that will enable them to be successful.

I've heard it said that "Character is who you are when no one else is around." That's a great definition!

If you're out fishing and you've caught your limit, but then you catch a bigger fish, do you throw away one of the smaller ones to fit the big one within your limit? Do you cheat on your taxes? If you found a hundred-dollar bill and no one was around to see you discover it, would you just pocket it? A man or woman of godly character, living a successful Christian lifestyle, does the *right thing* even when no one else (except God) would know. They do what's right because they are *righteous*.

If we've done our training job properly, our children will have a godly character even when we're not nearby to enforce righteous behavior.

The Bible offers such wisdom in the area of discipline. I would encourage you to use a concordance to review all the verses that mention discipline. But here I'd like to highlight just a few, to illustrate the various forms and purposes of discipline—why it's so important.

- Discipline is a necessary part of life. It keeps us on track and in God's will. People without discipline rarely accomplish anything in life and usually find themselves in one mess after another.

  *He will die for lack of discipline, led astray by his own great folly.*
  (PROV. 5:23)

- Discipline is one of our God-given responsibilities as parents, and it helps us to create a loving, peaceful home environment.

*"For I told him that I would judge his family forever because of the sin he knew about; his sons made themselves contemptible, and he failed to restrain them."*

(1 SAM. 3:13)

*Discipline your son, and he will give you peace; he will bring delight to your soul.*

(PROV. 29:17)

- When children are older, they learn self-discipline; but when they are young, they especially need the firm guidance of parents who have foresight to see the results of their actions and who wish to help their children develop a godly character.

  *A youngster's heart is filled with rebellion, but punishment will drive it out of him.*

  (PROV. 22:15, TLB)

- Through discipline, children gain wisdom and understanding. A key element of discipling is teaching through example, illustration, and also correction.

  *Whoever loves discipline loves knowledge, but he who hates correction is stupid.*

  (PROV. 12:1)

- Children must learn to obey God and their parents. Discipline teaches obedience and submission. Obedience to the Lord will lead to success and will free your child from the bondage of sin.

  *"Now then, my sons, listen to me; blessed are those who keep my ways."*

  (PROV. 8:32)

  *Direct my footsteps according to your word; let no sin rule over me.*

  (PS. 119:133)

  *Children, obey your parents in everything, for this pleases the Lord.*

  (COL. 3:20)

- Discipline comes from several sources: God, parents and self. Each one is vitally important. Hebrews explains the importance of discipline:

*Endure hardship as discipline; God is treating you as sons. For what son is not disciplined by his father? If you are not disciplined (and everyone undergoes discipline), then you are illegitimate children and not true sons. Moreover, we have all had human fathers who disciplined us and we respected them for it. How much more should we submit to the Father of our spirits and live! Our fathers disciplined us for a little while as they thought best; but God disciplines us for our good, that we may share in his holiness. No discipline seems pleasant at the time, but painful. Later on, however, it produces a harvest of righteousness and peace for those who have been trained by it.*

(HEB. 12:7-11)

Discipline is a vital and necessary component of the human parent/child relationship, just as it is in the relationship we have with God our Father. He disciplines us in order to lead us, correct us, teach us, and train us to be righteous.

When our children learn to submit to parental authority, they will then more easily be trained to submit to God's authority and discipline, and will eventually develop the self-discipline needed to lead a righteous life in obedience to the Lord.

That final step is vitally important—that our children learn *self-discipline*. Obedience is necessary primarily to avoid doing what is wrong. Self-discipline motivates the child to do what is right. See the difference? Sin is not just an action—something you *do*. Sin is *missing the mark*, not meeting God's standards. We sin when we fail to bring glory to God—failing to be in His will and to have an obedient attitude. Our motivation and action are extremely important. First Corinthians 10:31 tells us to bring glory to the Lord in *all* things ("whether you eat or drink"). Self-discipline is what enables us to live a Christian lifestyle and to keep God's glory as the guiding force in all of our thoughts, attitudes, play, work—everything we do, rather than just being a "legalistic" Christian.

## USING DISCIPLINE FOR CORRECTION

Your local Christian bookstore has many excellent resources available to assist you with the intricacies of correction and punishment. If you need further guidance, I encourage you to consult one of the Christian experts on this subject (one that is scripturally-based rather than dependent upon worldly psychology).

We don't have the room in this chapter to discuss the practicalities of correcting your children from diapers to dating. Nor will we discuss the current debate over spanking and proper techniques of spanking versus other punishments like "time out" (except to say I believe that spanking is a biblical concept [Proverbs 29:15], which is often taken to a counterproductive extreme in some households).

However, I would like to mention a few overriding scriptural principles to keep in mind as you select the method of correction that is best for your family.

First, *I encourage you to find a method of correction that follows biblical principles and focuses on discipleship beyond punishment*. All discipline should have a purpose for training and teaching, not just punishment for the sake of submission. Some of the biblical principles I ask you to consider are:

- *Consistency.* Inconsistent punishment loses its value and fails to teach. Your "no" ceases to mean anything if you often change your mind or give in to pressure.
- *Compassion and love.* When God dealt with His children and Jesus dealt with the disciples, compassion and love were clearly evident. Warnings were issued to the Israelites before judgment fell. They were given chances to repent and change their behavior.
- *Clear expectations.* The Bible clearly delineates acceptable and unacceptable behavior. We must do the same for our children.
- *Relevancy.* Punishment is most effective when it directly relates to the wrong behavior. For example, when we sin, our punishment is often the natural consequences of our sin.
- *Forgiveness.* After sin is dealt with, our Heavenly Father forgives us completely and wipes the slate clean. When punishing your child, resist the urge to resurrect past misbehaviors (the same principle applies to our marital arguments or discussions).
- *Reason.* Wouldn't it be awful if God changed the rules every day? Fortunately, He makes consistent sense, as should we. Clearly explain the wrong behavior to your child, the purpose for the punishment, and your expectations for his future behavior. Focus on the behavior rather than on negativity toward the child. It is helpful to stop and think before we react, asking ourselves these questions:

> Why was my child's behavior wrong?
> Was it really dangerous or sinful, or was it just a natural, childish behavior that was inconvenient to me?
> What was my child's motivation?

How can I best correct this specific behavior in order to encourage more positive actions in the future?

- *Steadfastness*. Our Lord's love is never-ceasing. We should never write our children off, give up on them, or think they're hopeless. Their behavior should never affect our love for them, and they should know that.
- *Planning and love*. Take a moment to cool down and reason with yourself rather than acting out your anger. Punishment should be for the good of the child, not for the good of the parent or to release steam.
- *Timeliness*. Discipline early and immediately. Correct the child right away before she forgets what she did wrong (this need is even more immediate in younger children). Begin discipline at an early age, as soon as they begin to understand. The longer you wait, the more negative behaviors they have developed, and the harder it will be to get them back on track. In the infinite wisdom of Proverbs 19:18, TLB we read:

> *Discipline your son in his early years while there is still hope. If you don't you will ruin his life.*

## HOW STRICT SHOULD I BE?

We all struggle with the dilemma of wanting to establish firm boundaries and yet being fearful of driving our children to rebellion. How do we walk this fine line?

I think my parents did an excellent job of this. They were never overly strict (in fact, I had more freedom than most of my friends); yet expectations were so clearly spelled out that I disciplined myself not to go beyond the limit. When I did make poor choices, I felt sad that I had let my parents down. They usually never had to say a thing; they could just look at me, and I would berate myself and apologize to them.

It's hard to say exactly how you can walk the line between authority and over-rigidity. This varies from household to household and depends a lot on the child's personality. Some children need firmer boundaries than others. But one basic principle applies: *as you train your children to be self-disciplined, it is necessary to gradually ease up on parental guidelines and let them hold themselves responsible for their own behavior.* This process is more commonly known as "becoming independent."

The parental "letting go" takes place slowly, in accordance with the child's age and maturity level. To be effective, a child's self-discipline must be developing accordingly. As the child becomes more responsible, he or she has fewer restrictions. The ability to show good self-management is rewarded with greater and greater freedoms.

The key that makes this transition possible is an open parent/child relationship that allows for ongoing modeling, teaching, and correction. A child must develop within an ever-widening circular boundary that is filled with love.

I like what popular youth speaker Dawson McAllister had to say in the Summer 1993 issue of *Marriage Partnership.* He told interviewer Ron Lee:

> Yes, it's possible to be too strict. That's why parents need to achieve a balance between the two requirements of good parenthood: The need to be consistent in enforcing the rules, while at the same time obeying God's command that we love our kids. When parents become too strict and the kid rebels even more, it's usually because the parents are failing to love the child with the same passion and level of dedication that they employ in disciplining the kid. You can't be a stickler on grades, curfew and being drug- and alcohol-free and expect it to work if you're not also listening to your kids, devoting a lot of time to them and getting involved in their lives. If you don't have love and discipline working hand-in-hand, your kids will probably get involved in things you don't want them involved in.
>
> I like this saying: "Rules only, without relationship, equals rebellion. Relationship only, without rules, equals chaos." Only God can show us how to balance those two contrasting statements and give our kids what they need from us.

## THE BALANCING ACT

Trying to correct and punish "just the right amount" is one of the toughest jobs in parenting. So much is at stake. We often feel like we're walking on a high-wire, trying to perfectly balance love and discipline.

The Bible reminds us of the important balance between obedience and encouragement:

> *Children, obey your parents in the Lord, for this is right. "Honor your father and mother"—which is the first commandment with a promise— "that it may go well with you and that you may enjoy long life on the*

*earth." Fathers, do not exasperate your children; instead, bring them up in the training and instruction of the Lord.*

(EPH. 6:1-4)

We clearly see the importance of obedience, which usually comes only through some correction. Yet, Paul immediately reminds us not to go too far. I like the way the correlating verse in Colossians 3:21 expresses this idea: "Fathers, do not embitter your children, or they will be discouraged."

None of us want exasperated, embittered, discouraged children! That's why discipline must go beyond punishment and focus on discipleship—"instead, bring them up in the training and instruction of the Lord."

How can you communicate these important ideas to your family? First, instruct them in the verses we just covered. Then initiate a family discussion in which you examine the roles and responsibilities of each member of the family. These roles come in three areas: 1) in the household work; 2) in relationship to one another; 3) as God instructs.

In Chapter 16's Family Night lesson, we studied the various talents we bring to the family as a part of the body. A discussion on roles and responsibilities as part of the body will continue to encourage our children to fulfill their roles, using the unique talents and traits God has given each of them, and will encourage them to take responsibility for fulfilling these roles.

Point out the reward God gives to children who honor their parents; then discuss what honor means and how it can be done on a practical, day-to-day basis.

Now for the balancing side. We've encouraged our children to obey the Lord and fulfill their home responsibilities and honor their parents. Now it's time to work on ourselves. We need to ask our children what kinds of things make them feel exasperated or angry.

If my child feels like I keep nagging him to clean his room, does that mean I just give up asking him? No. But it points out the necessity to discuss the situation and find another way to accomplish the goal without exasperating or discouraging my son. When we discuss this calmly as a family, we can help the children reach their own conclusion that if they would obey the first time they are asked, we wouldn't need to ask again. Perhaps a cause-and-effect relationship needs to be introduced. If the room isn't clean, he can't have anyone over to play or go play with anyone else until it is done. I don't have to say a word. The expectation is clear. It may take a few days of boredom, but eventually it will work.

Perhaps your daughter doesn't like being told what she must wear in the morning, and yet you know she'll choose something unsuitable for the weather if left to her own devices. Your family discussion may lead to an agreement that she'll be given three choices but must pick one of them without complaining.

Honor and non-exasperation work together, mutually contributing to a peaceful atmosphere in the home. However, they are not dependent upon each other. Like God's instructions to husbands and wives, even if one person is failing to hold up their end of the bargain, the other still has a responsibility to the Lord to do as He instructs. Just as parents cannot say, "My child does not honor me, and therefore I must exasperate him," the child cannot say, "My mom is bugging me, and therefore I don't have to honor what she is saying."

You may want to consider having the honor/exasperation family meeting every month, to review how things are working and to come to new solutions as a family, so that all of you can obey the Lord and hold up your end of the family bargain.

As challenging as it often may seem, it's part of our job as parents to come up with creative solutions to our own family's unique situations. No one said parenting is easy! Sometimes it takes many tries before you'll find something that works with your own kids. The Bible is, of course, a great source of inspiration for ideas. *The Living Bible* version of Ephesians 6:4 emphasizes the need for such discussions and solutions:

> *And now a word to you parents. Don't keep on scolding and nagging your children, making them angry and resentful. Rather, bring them up with the loving discipline the Lord himself approves, with suggestions and godly advice.*

## THE IMPORTANCE OF SELF-DISCIPLINE

Ultimately, the most important area of discipling your child is in the area of self-management. Becoming responsible and self-disciplined in obedience to the Lord will put your child on auto-pilot and cause him or her to make good decisions and be successful as an adult.

Oh, that our children would be so eager as David to cry out:

*Search me, O God, and know my heart; test me and know my anxious thoughts. See if there is any offensive way in me, and lead me in the way everlasting.*

(Ps. 139:23-24)

I want my own family to operate that way—being so desirous to do God's will that we are concerned about those things of which we're not even aware. We are in the most important race ever, and only self-discipline that pushes us to serve God with every ounce of our being will enable us to win the prize. Paul talks of this race:

*Do you not know that in a race all the runners run, but only one gets the prize? Run in such a way as to get the prize. Everyone who competes in the games goes into strict training. They do it to get a crown that will not last; but we do it to get a crown that will last forever. Therefore I do not run like a man running aimlessly; I do not fight like a man beating the air. No, I beat my body and make it my slave so that after I have preached to others, I myself will not be disqualified for the prize.*

(1 Cor. 9:24-27)

Paul tells us that self-discipline is vitally important if we are to be successful in winning the race of life. We race not for worldly prizes of money, fame, and power (a crown that will not last), but for an eternal crown that will last forever—the glory of being in God's presence and sharing in His holiness. This eternal success will result from self-discipline.

Self-discipline, and the race for the eternal crown, often involve self-sacrifice. Paul tells us:

*Take your share of suffering as a good soldier of Jesus Christ, just as I do, and as Christ's soldier do not let yourself become tied up in worldly affairs, for then you cannot satisfy the one who has enlisted you in his army. Follow the Lord's rules for doing his work, just as an athlete either follows the rules or is disqualified and wins no prize. Work hard, like a farmer who gets paid well if he raises a large crop. . . . I am comforted by this truth, that when we suffer and die for Christ it only means that we will begin living with him in heaven. And if we think that our present service for him is hard, just remember that some day we are going to sit with him and rule with him. But if we give up when we suffer, and turn against Christ, then he must turn against us. Even when we are too weak to have any faith left, he remains faithful to us and will help us,*

*for he cannot disown us who are part of himself, and he will always carry out his promises to us.*
(2 Tim. 2:3-6, 11-13, TLB)

Self-discipline requires *obedience* to the Lord. We must follow His rules. It requires *perseverance and a proper focus.* We probably will not receive earthly rewards, but our eternal crown is more than worth it. And it requires *faithfulness.* Christ promises to be faithful to us and to strengthen us; we must remain faithful to Him. These are many of the same ingredients required for success. Self-discipline is essential to success.

A disciplined person:

- Keeps on going when others have dropped out.
- Finds success in "cans" rather than "can'ts."
- Doesn't need someone looking over his shoulder, because his shoulder is pressed against the next obstacle to achievement.

Self-discipline will also enable your children to resist temptation, because they will depend on God and obey His Word. First Corinthians 10:13 tells us:

*No temptation has seized you except what is common to man. And God is faithful; he will not let you be tempted beyond what you can bear. But when you are tempted, he will also provide a way out so that you can stand up under it.*

When we are self-disciplined, with our focus on the Lord, we can resist external pressures that threaten to tempt us to go astray or take our attention away from things of the Lord.

Self-discipline also allows us to fit more things into our day. When we are disciplined, our lives are more organized and less chaotic. Julie Andrews says:

Some people regard discipline as a chore. For me, it is a kind of order that sets me free to fly.

True, self-discipline is work, like anything else worthwhile in life. But the time spent in developing self-discipline is more than paid back in the time it frees up once you have mastered it.

On the downside, self-discipline can give one a false sense of self-control, or the illusion of having complete control over your own life;

so the temptation is to fit in more worldly activities. But we know that we truly don't control our own lives. To be successful, we must submit our lives to the Lord. So first and foremost, self-discipline must be used to become a *godly* success.

> But seek ye first the kingdom of God, and his righteousness; and all these things shall be added unto you.
> (MATT. 6:33, KJV)

To be successful, we must use our self-discipline to put God first in everything—including our time. Many of us, beginning to do this as adults, have found that having the self-discipline for study time each morning, consistently, is quite a challenge. But we've seen how a quiet, intimate time with God each day will set us on the right track.

It's funny, but whenever I think I don't have enough time for my quiet study time with the Lord, I can never complete the other goals for my day either. But when I decide that seeking God is my *first* priority, and I spend that time, no matter how rushed my day may promise to be, the Lord seems to give that time back to me. When I make time with God my first priority, I am somehow always able to get everything else done in my day. And with a much better attitude!

It's just like tithing. When I think I don't have enough money and decide to skip my tithe, I invariably have a terrible month financially. However, when I make tithing my first priority (even if it seems that's all the money there is), I am always able to meet my other financial obligations.

It's so true. What we give to the Lord with a pure heart, we receive back full and overflowing. This is as true of our time as of our money. Time spent with the Lord is never wasted.

We can instill in our children the important self-discipline of seeking God first. Self-discipline is best learned at an early age, when it becomes as natural and automatic as brushing one's teeth. This gift to your child will make self-discipline, and spiritual self-discipline, easier as an adult. Perhaps if you struggle with the challenge now, you wish your own parents had made spiritual self-discipline a natural part of your life. With a young child you can start with just a verse and a simple prayer each morning or each night. An older child can read a passage or chapter on her own each morning or at bedtime.

When I was young, I developed this habit in my own life. I always read at least a chapter of my Bible before going to sleep. This simple activity put me on auto-pilot in a way that may have saved my spiritual life. Even when I went through times of rebellion and sin and felt very far away from God, I would read a chapter of the Bible each night. I tried not to, because the Lord convicted me through His Word. But I literally could not sleep without reading—just as I could not fall asleep without brushing my teeth. Through this deeply ingrained habit, my Heavenly Father held on to me when I could easily have drifted away.

When I let go of Him, He never let go of me. Self-discipline, which I'd been taught since I was a small child, was the vehicle through which God spoke to me when I wasn't listening. Though hard to develop at first (especially for an adult), self-discipline eventually becomes very easy. In fact, it becomes a way of life, a habit. And it's a powerful force for putting your children on auto-pilot. I know it was for me.

## Bringing It Home

*Applying God's Principles: Please refer to Chapter 2 for ideas on Family Night format and activities.*

Opening:    What are some definitions of *discipline?*

Scripture:    Proverbs 6:20-23; Proverbs 1:8.

Discussion:    Why should children listen to their parents' instruction? How will it benefit them? Why is discipline important? Why are parents to discipline their children?

Application:    1. Discuss any recent or ongoing discipline problems in the family. How can these be resolved by children honoring their parents and parents not discouraging the children?

2. Have each child discuss situations where he or she feels "nagged." Use creative ideas to resolve these situations to the satisfaction of everyone involved.

3. Have each child choose one area in which he or she would like to become more self-disciplined. Form a plan of action to make this possible.

# CHAPTER 19

◆

# *Responsible Self-management*

The United States is based on the principle of self-government—each person governing his own actions.

> We have staked the whole future of American civilization, not upon the power of government, far from it. We have staked the future of all political institutions upon the capacity of mankind for self-government; upon the capacity of each and all of us to govern ourselves, to sustain ourselves according to the Ten Commandments of God. (James Madison, "the father of the Constitution")

Wouldn't it be wonderful if we could eventually get our families to function that way (more effectively than our country, of course)! In fact, that's the way God's people should operate—each one responsible to the Lord for his or her own behaviors and choices. Ultimately, we are accountable to the Lord for everything that takes place in our lives.

## SELF-MANAGEMENT

God gives us talents and abilities to develop and use, not to waste. He directs my life, but I am accountable to manage it. We have the freedom to choose not to obey. Our goal is to train our children to *choose* to obey the Lord.

As James Madison stated, the success of our country depends upon each citizen's ability for self-management, as does the success of each individual's life. Self-management is the key to achieving anything.

God wants each of us to succeed. He gave us His Spirit to live in us to insure our success—to enable us to be the persons He intended and to live lives that produce fruit and are salt and light to others and to the world.

God has given each of us the capacity to succeed in living our life for Him. Yet each of us is responsible for making choices, decisions, and commitments to work for Him and to do His will—to make the most of the life He has given us.

When a child who is responsibly self-managing his life looks at goals or something he or she is supposed to do, he'll have an attitude that positively states, "I can!"—"I will!"—"I did!"

Each person must set his or her own goals, establish a plan, and take persistent action; in other words, each person must manage the course of his or her life. We are stewards of our time on earth, just as we are stewards of our finances. God controls it; we manage it. God has placed in us the desire to achieve, and He expects us to put that desire to work for His glory.

Since self-management is the key to achieving anything, it is a key concept for children to grasp. It is never too early or too late to start teaching self-management to your sons and daughters. It will enable them to take initiative and responsibility for the direction of their lives.

It is also important that children learn self-management *under God's government*. Under God's government we know that He has a plan for each of us. He has also set standards for us to live by and has blessings in store for us. It is the responsibility of each one of us, under His government, to manage ourselves by committing our way to the Lord. We must let His Spirit and His Word guide our decisions, commitments, and actions; and we must allow Him to produce success in our lives.

Self-discipline allows me to feel a sense of control in my life and to manage my life more efficiently and effectively. But I must always remember that my own management, my own self-discipline, is *secondary to God's management*. I use it only as a tool to be more effective in obeying Him. I must submit my own goals, plans, and desires to His will for my life.

We can teach our children these points as we help them to understand that God governs and directs us. We manage our lives; we are accountable to Him. These two truths are connected by our personal relationship with the Lord through His Son, Jesus Christ. Because of Christ, we have rapport with God, and we can communicate with Him. It is a relationship marked by harmony, accord, and conformity.

## ENCOURAGING RESPONSIBILITY IN YOUR CHILD

As a child learns to manage his life under God's government, he learns that he must make commitments regarding what God has given him in all areas of life. He (or she) learns that his responsibility is his *response* to his God-given abilities. Every parent would like their child to be responsible, but what are some practical ways we can encourage the development of this trait in our children?

Responsibility is cultivated by goal-setting and achievement. A child must cross the bridge from external discipline to internal discipline.

*External discipline* clearly influences the child's life as it comes from parents, teachers, the church, and our laws. Children learn to follow the rules with the threat of being punished in some way or in an effort to "get what they want." *Internal discipline* is a little harder to cultivate. The child must develop responsibility within him- or herself. Internal discipline is guided by desires, plans, and commitments.

Parental expectation is important in helping a child develop self-discipline. Children learn responsibility best when they are called upon to be responsible. That is *training*, not just teaching! If a child is not expected to act responsibly and accomplish the goals set out, chances are he won't.

Children need reminders more than they need to be told. Once they have been taught what is expected of them, further teaching isn't necessary. However, training is still needed; and it effectively comes in the form of reminding the child of your expectations. Here are some ideas to help them remember their responsibilities without your nagging them:

- *Put a bulletin board* on their door for notes. Put up notes of encouragement and affirmation as well as reminders.
- *Help your children develop a list of goals* and a list of steps to take toward achieving each goal. Use this list as a reminder, and cross off items completed to help your child feel a sense of accomplishment (or put gold stars next to items completed).

- *Give each child a large calendar* for hanging near his or her desk at home.
- *Give each child a pocket calendar* for recording assignments.
- *Teach your child to always look back when leaving a place* and ask, "Am I forgetting anything?"

## HELPING YOUR CHILD SET GOALS

Learning to set goals will enable your child to be more self-disciplined and to better manage his or her own life. It's critical that children learn to be responsible for their God-given abilities. By setting goals in all areas of life, a child can focus on priorities and evaluate her direction based on God's government or God's will.

Goals are important for self-disciplined learning as well as for a self-disciplined life. For now, here are some of the important benefits your children will gain as they become more responsible and learn self-discipline by setting goals for their lives:

- They will translate God's values and purposes into daily life.
- They will learn to take initiative.
- They will learn to be accountable.
- They will learn how to succeed day by day.
- They will learn how to handle obstacles and setbacks.
- They will gain a sense of power and control in their lives (strength through the Lord and control submitted to His guidance).
- They will learn organizational skills necessary for achievement.
- They will learn leadership skills.

Goals can be set with children of any age. For a very young child, goals may include such activities as brushing teeth or picking up toys. For older children, goals advance to finishing homework and washing the car.

Parents can make a chart that lists the child's goals (tasks) down the left side of the paper and the days of the week across the top. Each goal can be checked off as it is accomplished each day. Individual goals may fall under sections like:

- "How I Take Care of Myself" (examples: brush teeth, wash face, wash hands, earn money).
- "How I Take Care of My Things" (examples: make bed, pick up toys, hang up clothes, do homework, put away games and sports equipment).

- "How I Help Others" (examples: set the table, take out the trash, clear the table, vacuum, dust, help wash dishes, feed the dog).

Parents can reinforce goal accomplishment with external rewards such as a trip to the park, a small toy, or a favorite meal when the child has accumulated a certain number of checks or accomplishments. However, studies have shown that when external rewards are used:

- The smallest possible reward should be used.
- The reward should only be used until the activity is mastered (a seven-year-old would not be rewarded for brushing his teeth in the same way that a three-year-old would).
- Rewards are best if unexpected rather than held out as a bribe.

While the use of external rewards can be helpful (businesses use them to motivate employees all the time!), their primary appeal to the child is that they represent approval, a pat on the back. But if relied upon too heavily, external rewards can backfire, causing children to work *only* when offered a reward.

The theory of external rewards is based on Pavlov's psychological studies on manipulating animals, which I myself find distasteful, although many well-known Christian parenting experts endorse the technique. We must remember that our children are *not* animals; they are capable of far more complex reasoning.

Personally, I think it is better to use less tangible external rewards that are unexpected, like a favorite meal, a gold star or smiley-face sticker, a big hug and a word of appreciation, or an actual pat on the back. Your loving verbal reminders can encourage a more effective form of reward—the intrinsic reward. Help your child become aware of:

- His sense of accomplishment for completing the task.
- Her sense of freedom now that her responsibilities are taken care of.
- Naturally occurring rewards and the good feeling they invoke inside. For example: someone was helped, money was earned, the cleaned room looks good and is more pleasant to live in, a parent is pleased with the child's performance, a parent no longer "nags," etc.

It is most effective to have the child help in developing his own list of goals. Here are some guidelines to remember when setting goals:

- To stimulate your child's thoughts in developing her own goals, *use the following list of verbs*: to go, to do, to see, to own, to learn, to read, to play, to be, to make, to earn, to save, to help, to give, to build.

- *Goals should be realistic.* He or she must believe it is possible to achieve given his or her experience, age, and degree of confidence. Goals become unrealistic when not enough time is given to accomplish the goal, when there are too many goals to accomplish at once, or when there is no desire to accomplish the goal.
- *Goals must be achievable.* If a goal seems too large or unmanageable, help your child break it down into smaller "baby steps." It may be helpful to think about the resources needed to reach the goal, obstacles that may be encountered and must be overcome, and the benefits of reaching the goal.
- *Define the goal specifically*, with a specific outcome and specific steps to reach the goal.
- *Goals must be relevant*, of interest to the child. The child must understand *why* he wants to achieve the goal.
- *Goals must be in line with God's plan.* Children must be taught to act responsibly, not just according to their own desires. Teach them to pray about their goals and to ask for guidance in their plans.
- *Goals must always be submitted to God's calling.* Sometimes we can set our own goals, but God may decide He has other plans for us; we need to be flexible and sensitive to His leading. However, while this may be a valid reason, it shouldn't be used as an excuse for unaccomplished goals.
- *Goals should have a specific time frame* in which they will be completed.
- *Goals must be measurable.* If a child says, "I will be nicer to my friends," how can this goal be measured to see if the child has succeeded? Perhaps by less arguments, she doesn't cause the friend to cry, etc.

## THE IMPORTANCE OF FAMILY GOALS

As we've learned, the most effective method of training our children is modeling. One way you can get your child excited about setting and achieving his own goals is to set family goals.

As each new year begins, my husband and I set goals for our family. Some of these are for us, some for the entire family, others for each of us as an individual. We cover ten major areas, including spiritual, financial, marriage, family development, social, professional, physical and health, hobbies, service/involvement, and travel. We begin and end by praying for God to lead us in our goals, then to help us accomplish them and keep us submitted to His will.

In each of these areas we set just a few major goals for the coming year. Some goals are easy to put into effect immediately; for example, we need to resume attending the Wednesday night Bible study at our church, and we need to buy life insurance.

Other goals need to be broken down into smaller steps. For example, we set a goal to pay off some costs incurred with a recent move and remodeling. This required evaluating our present condition, evaluating upcoming needs, developing a realistic timeline, developing a budget that would enable us to pay off these costs, and then actually beginning the process.

I believe the entire family can be involved in all family goals. For instance, under marriage we decided to have a firm Friday date night. While this is a goal *for us*, the entire family needs to accept this type of goal and accommodate it. By making our budget a family matter, we can teach our children the process and value of budgeting. When you set family goals, your children may just get so enthusiastic that they will want to set their own goals.

It is then valuable to review the family goals each week at a specified time (perhaps as part of Family Night or during a specific meal). This will help you keep on track and will also model to your children the intrinsic rewards you reap as goals are accomplished (there is no extrinsic reward for meeting most family goals).

Family goals can be a lot of fun as well as a terrific learning experience. Just one note of caution: parents must be responsible to meet their goals. These are not New Year's resolutions to be discarded within a few weeks. If you fail to meet the goals, you are modeling the exact opposite of self-discipline to your children! Family goals are also, then, a great accountability mechanism for us parents!

Success comes when our God-given abilities are coupled with the proper motivation and self-discipline. All three ingredients must be included for success to occur. Someone with all the ability in the world will never be a godly success if they don't use it properly (have the right motivation). Nor will they be a success, even if they really want to do God's will, if they don't have the self-discipline and responsibility to carry the plan through to completion.

If we wish for our children to be successful, we must train them well in all three essentials: *skills and abilities, motivation and obedience*, and *self-discipline*.

## Bringing It Home

*Applying God's Principles: Please refer to Chapter 2 for ideas on Family Night format and activities.*

Opening:      Why should you develop responsibility and self-discipline?

Scripture:      1 Corinthians 9:24-27.

Discussion:      What is the race referred to in this passage? Since Paul says he is not "running aimlessly," what is the goal or finish line toward which he's running? What does it mean to make your body a slave to your efforts rather than being a slave to your body's desires?

Application:     
1. Compare this passage to a sports competition or contest that your child has personally experienced. What preparation or self-discipline was necessary to succeed?

2. What was the prize offered in that competition? Contrast this to the eternal crown of which Paul speaks. Which is more valuable?

3. How can we discipline ourselves to run a good race? How can setting goals help us?

4. Have each child set one goal for the week. Break it down into action steps. What will be the reward? (Compare intrinsic rewards with the eternal crown in Paul's illustration.)

# CHAPTER 20

◆

# *Study Skills: Keys to Learning*

To be successful, our children must develop and use the talents and abilities God gave them to glorify Him. The first step in this process is learning—learning to read and write, learning about the Lord and His will by studying the Bible, and becoming self-disciplined and organized so that they can *use* this knowledge appropriately.

I've known many a bright child with excellent potential who simply couldn't succeed because he or she lacked basic study skills. They lacked the ability to organize and use material properly, and their plans failed because they failed to plan. You may know adults who fit this description.

Study skills are not only useful in getting your child through school or helping him to pass the next test (though academic achievement is an important benefit). Good study skills have carried me throughout my career, in life pursuits (such as organizing the remodeling of our home), and most importantly in spiritual growth. Good study skills will directly or indirectly impact the success of *every area* of your child's life.

While many schools attempt to teach these important skills, I believe they must be taught and reinforced at home. Study skills can't be developed in a one-week unit; consistent monitoring and reminders are necessary. Most teachers simply do not have the time to provide students with this individual reinforcement. You can best provide this encouragement at home. Like anything repeated over time, your child will eventually make a habit of planning and being organized when you consistently encourage and teach these skills.

What are study skills? We will look briefly at several aspects, offering some practical tips for teaching these skills to your child. If you need more information, consult your local librarian for additional instructional materials on skill development. In an earlier chapter we covered reading, one of the most important study skills for your child. In this chapter we will look at the following:

- Planning.
- Time management.
- Organization.
- Writing.
- Study strategies.

## START WITH A PLAN

Planning can be short-term or long-term. When my husband and I set our goals for the year, those were long-term plans (we have even longer, five-year goals as well). When you decide to take a trip to Europe in six months, you form a long-term plan that involves saving money, making reservations, choosing sightseeing destinations, etc. Long-term plans usually involve multiple goals or goals with many steps.

The ability to set goals is vitally important to your child's future success. In the last chapter we explained how to set achievable goals.

A study of Harvard alumni showed that ten years after graduation those with written goals earned ten times as much as those with no goals. Even those with unwritten but specific goals earned three times as much as those without goals. I use this illustration not to say money is what's important, but to show you the importance of goals, especially written ones.

Goals keep us focused on our plan, and therefore we are more likely to achieve them. This applies to spiritual plans for success as well as academic and professional goals. *Most of the time, when our plans fail, it is because we have failed to plan!*

Short-term plans cover a condensed duration, like a day or a week. They often look more like a "to do" list. I'm a real list-maker myself. I've found that the practice of keeping lists overcomes three major obstacles to my success:

- Lists keep me focused on daily priorities.
- Lists prevent me from forgetting tasks.
- Lists free my mind to concentrate on individual tasks or to be creative.

After I write down my plans, I can "forget" about them. I just have to remember to look at my list after each task I complete! I've found that organizing my plans enables me to accomplish about ten times what I get done when I'm not organized and sticking to a plan. Now, instead of getting overwhelmed by all the things I need to do, I write them all down (even the details), then forget the "big picture" and concentrate my attention on the first priority at hand. What a stress reliever!

The Bible encourages us to plan. In fact, the Bible reveals *God's plan* to us. His plan gives us life. Proverbs 29:18 (KJV) says:

> *Where there is no vision, the people perish; but he that keepeth the law, happy is he.*

Through His Word, the Lord also gives us some great wisdom that we should keep in mind when making our own plans:

> *Plans fail for lack of counsel, but with many advisers they succeed.*
> (PROV. 15:22)

> *There is no wisdom, no insight, no plan that can succeed against the* LORD.
> (PROV. 21:30)

> *In his heart a man plans his course, but the* LORD *determines his steps.*
> (PROV. 16:9)

When we make our plans, we should seek counsel from others, especially if our plans involve them or if we are setting major life goals. We should also seek counsel from the Lord, since all our plans must be submitted to His will if they are to succeed.

You can help your child learn these important concepts, using the following process:

- Help him or her develop a list of things that must be done the next day or during the next week (i.e., homework assignments, working toward the completion of a term project, studying for a test, sports activities and practices, chores, etc.). As the child gets older and develops skill in planning, your assistance should taper off.

- Together, go over the list. Offer any input you may have. Strategize how to overcome any obstacles that might arise. (You are the "adviser.")
- Take the plans to the Lord in prayer. Pray that He will enable the child to accomplish his goals, overcome any obstacles, and learn from any failures. Submit the plans to Him, that His will be done.
- Help your child to prioritize his or her plans, listing the most important ones at the top or placing a star next to them. These should be addressed first.

When you help your child prioritize her plans, it may be helpful to address her motivation. Ask her why she places top priority on a certain task. We should apply the "motivation test" to long-term goals as well. For instance, if your teenager is deciding upon a career or where to pursue his education, encourage him to ask himself or herself these questions: *Is my motivation to gain prestige by my educational degrees? Is it to become rich? Or am I pursuing this plan to enable me to further serve the Lord and minister to people?*

The motivation behind your child's plans will reveal his view of success. What is the most important thing for him to pursue? Certainly one doesn't have to go into formal ministry to serve the Lord. We can glorify Him in any position in which He places us. But if the child wants to become a doctor, is it for the money, the prestige, or to help people?

While the child's motivation is very important, his or her *lack of motivation* can also be a hindrance to planning. Many children simply see planning as "too hard," "too time-consuming," or "a hassle." Many adults have similar complaints (perhaps even yourself!). Yes, planning takes a little more time up front; but I can assure you, it's more efficient in the long run. If you don't believe me, just try it for two weeks (really try, and follow through on your plans). I think you'll see my point.

You can encourage your unmotivated child in the same way. Develop a short-term "trial" so he can see how planning will benefit him. With an unmotivated child, it's best to practice the planning process on a goal he really wants to achieve—perhaps to earn money to buy a certain toy. Once he sees how well the system works, he'll be more inclined to apply it to other areas where accomplishment is needed, such as schoolwork.

How far ahead should you help your children plan? This varies with the age of the child. Younger children have a shorter attention span and memory. They need very short-term plans with a quicker "payoff" (seeing results). They also respond well to more tangible rewards. A toddler can focus best on plans for the next hour or two, but probably not for more than a day. For instance, you might form a plan for the next hour—"First we'll pick up these toys in your room; then we'll run by the dry cleaner for Mommy; then we'll go to the park." Such a young child needs to have a positive experience to look forward to, such as going to the park. This makes the mundane more easily tolerated. Keep the string of tasks short, and stick to your promises. This will reinforce the positive nature of planning.

As a child gets older, in grade school, he or she can look forward to planning for the week. At this time it's helpful to follow the steps I outlined earlier, to make a weekly plan each Sunday night. It still helps to have a tangible, positive outcome when the goals are completed. For example, "If we stick to this plan, you'll have all your homework completed by Friday night. Then you'll be able to play during the weekend and go to that baseball game you wanted to see on Saturday night."

As children mature, they lengthen their forward-looking capabilities and are able to plan for a quarter or even for a year. This type of planning is necessary when teachers begin assigning term projects. Finally, by the time students are in their junior and senior years of high school, they must start planning for the future, at least two to four years ahead, in selecting a college at which to pursue their vocation or in planning long-term to decide if they are better off going directly into the work world.

It's important to remember that even when planning for longer spans of time, goals must be broken down into smaller steps in order to organize the plan for optimal achievement.

*Modeling* provides a great way for you to encourage your children to plan. Take advantage of this powerful force! You make many plans each day and each week—many of them subconsciously, since planning becomes a habit.

By being aware as you make plans, even minor ones, you can verbally model them to your children. For example, each morning discuss your plan for the day. As you begin a certain task, even one as simple as the laundry, outline your plan to your young children. Children love to be involved in weekly meal planning. Let them help select meals, from among choices, then develop a shopping list. Then as you actually prepare a meal, verbally think through the steps you use in scheduling the preparation of the food so it's ready on time.

## TIME MANAGEMENT

The important skill of time management enables us to efficiently plan our days and make the most of our time. In the food preparation example above, you would use time management skills to decide when to begin preparing each dish so the entire dinner would be ready at the same time. As you teach your children to plan, be sure to include the vital component of time management.

Making sure our plans can be accomplished in the time allotted and determining our priorities based on the time we have available are key elements of the planning process. Let's add another step to the method we outlined earlier to help your child develop a plan for the following day or week:

- Help your child determine the amount of time necessary to complete each task and allocate his hours accordingly. For example, if he gets home from school at 2, then works on homework for an hour until 3, then has soccer practice from 4:30 to 6, which task can he plan on completing between 3 and 4:30? Perhaps he could allow an hour to wash the dog, then half an hour to rest and have a snack before practice.

*The keys to time management are proper planning of our schedule and balance.* Scheduling can be done easily by using a calendar that shows time blocks for the day, then fitting items from our planning list into available blocks of time.

I'm not saying we should schedule our children's days like a military school or expect them to be productive 100 percent of the time. They need plenty of time simply to be children. But time management is an important skill to be learned and utilized *when things must be accomplished*—for example, schoolwork, chores, projects, etc. Not every hour, or even every day, has to be full of plans. The challenge is to help your child see planning as fun and useful. Those of us who are natural organizers have to be careful not to overdo it!

The second key element—balance—also ties in with priorities. As we make our plans and as we schedule our time, we must keep our priorities in mind and balance our time. Ephesians 5:15-16 tells us:

*Be very careful, then, how you live—not as unwise but as wise, making the most of every opportunity, because the days are evil.*

We must plan our time with an eternal focus, allowing our desire for godly success to help us determine our priorities. In this area we should keep a couple of basics in mind:

- We must help our children understand (and realize this ourselves, as well!) that *an activity for God is not a substitute for a relationship with God.* Going to church on Sunday, or even to a Bible study, is not enough. We need to read the Word and be in prayerful communication with our Heavenly Father.
- *Be sure to schedule time for rest and relaxation!* God rested on the seventh day. We don't want to be efficient and effective for one month and then burn out; we're in this for the long haul!
- *Take time to smell the roses!* It's easy to get so caught up in tasks that we forget to live! Enjoy the beauty of God's creation; take time to be still and know that He is God; laugh with your family and friends. Don't forget to have fun!

If we keep our priorities in focus with the Lord and plan our time in a balanced way, we will enhance our own lives and will help our children to be happier. Our goal is to be efficient and effective and always joyful in the Lord—not to be obsessed or neurotic!

Columnist Dolores Curran addressed the importance of this concept in the Spring 1993 issue of *Marriage Partnership.* A frustrated parent of an overinvolved fifteen-year-old wrote in for advice, voicing a common ailment that you may have experienced yourself. The mother wrote, "We want her to maximize her God-given talents, but we also want to maintain a realistic family schedule. As it is, we're beginning to get worn out by all of her rehearsals, concerts, recitals and other extracurricular activities."

Curran responded, emphasizing the need for balance within the daughter's life and within the family activities. I'd like to share her practical suggestion, since this problem is a common one today. Curran wrote:

One of your tasks as parents is to help your daughter learn to get control of her life while all of you maintain a healthy family life. At 15, she doesn't yet understand that she can't do everything she wants to do. And, being typically egocentric at this age, she doesn't feel a great responsibility toward the rest of the family.

I suggest that you and your spouse settle on an appropriate number of hours your daughter can spend per week on her activities without endangering her health and the wellbeing of the family. Then allow her to choose the activities on which she will spend these hours.

This limitation will force her to prioritize, a skill many of us learned only later in life. We are seeing more and more signs of stress and burnout in children, whereas these were once reserved to adults. In fact, it's the kind of compulsiveness you cite in your daughter than often leads to anorexia, perfectionism and depression in adolescents.

As much as we like our children to excel and to be happy, all of their God-given talents do not have to be experienced and mastered within one or two years. You have a right, also, to sanity and a healthy family life, so you have a responsibility to help your daughter get her activities under control. She will resist this, of course, but I hope you stay firm, for the sake of your entire family.

## HELPING YOUR CHILD GET ORGANIZED

Being organized in every area of life is helpful, but the most important area in which we can help our children get organized is with their schoolwork. Once they become accustomed to organizing their assignments and projects, they'll see the value in organizing their personal and spiritual pursuits and eventually their professional life. Here are some ways you can help your child achieve at school by becoming more organized:

- Give your child a *pocket calendar*, where he can note upcoming tests and assignments. Be sure it has plenty of room in the back where your child can make lists of assignments, items needed for class, reminders of things to ask Mom or Dad, etc. This will reinforce *planning*.
- If your child has term projects, help her to *plot her plan*, broken down into small chunks, in the pocket calendar, so that tasks can be completed gradually over the course of the term and cause less stress to the family. This will help teach *time management*.
- Help your child *organize the instruments needed* for class (pencil, pen, paper, ruler, highlighters, calculator, etc.). Keep these items in special places (i.e., a certain pocket of a backpack or an organizer

with pockets), so they are always easily accessible when needed. Keep schoolwork in a special location in your child's room so it can easily be found when she is ready to leave for school in the morning. When you sign papers, always put them back in the special location for her to return, along with her lunch or lunch money. This prevents forgetting things and teaches *responsibility*.

- Help your child *plan ahead for tests*. Be sure material is read and highlighted, study cards made and studied, etc., well ahead of time, then reviewed the night before and the morning of the test. Be sure your child has a healthy, balanced breakfast and wears comfortable clothing, so there will be no distractions during the test. An extra encouraging word from Mom and Dad goes a long way too! Excellent books are available on test-taking strategies if you need them, but being *organized and prepared* is the key to success!

## WRITING SKILLS

Imagine how hard it would be to function in life if you couldn't write. Writing skills are as vitally important as reading skills; we can't communicate effectively without them. In all the suggestions I've made thus far in this chapter, writing has served a key purpose: writing down our goals, making lists, plotting our plan on a calendar, organizing our time. Writing will also be a key to effective study strategies.

There are many kinds of writing:

- Academic (papers, essays, tests).
- Note-taking.
- Professional.
- Social.
- Personal business correspondence.
- Filling out forms.
- Practical communication (leaving notes for other family members, making lists, etc.).
- Creative and therapeutic.
- Spiritual study.

Your child will undoubtedly use each type within the course of his or her life. How well your child communicates in writing may be the key to future success in graduating from school and obtaining and maintaining employment.

Writing is not a task in and of itself. It's intricately woven into the thinking process. Words come from the mind. To be effective in communicating, they must be clear, coherent, and organized. You can encourage your child to develop these skills by creating opportunities for him to write. Here are a few ideas to consider:

- A thank-you note or letter to Grandma.
- A list of things he'd like for Christmas.
- "To do" lists.
- A personal diary.
- A story to accompany the picture he drew.
- A different ending to a story he's read.

Be sure to give your child plenty of time to write and a place where he or she can think clearly. Your child will learn to enjoy writing much more if you provide "real things" for him to write rather than making up artificial assignments. Focus on something he is interested in, perhaps something he's read about, that will stimulate ideas.

It may help your child get started if you ask him some questions. For instance, if he is writing a letter to Grandma, you might ask, "What have you been doing lately? How did that make you feel? Who did you do it with? What exciting things are coming up? Where will you be going?" Remember the basic who, what, when, where, how, and why—essential stimuli for writing.

It takes a lot of practice to learn to write well. You can help your child develop this skill by providing lots of opportunities, encouragement, and feedback—both positive and constructive (be careful not to discourage him or her, though). By asking questions (rather than making negative comments), you can help your child see areas where he or she can expand and revise his or her first draft to improve it. If you get your child into the habit of writing at least two or three drafts before the final version, he or she won't feel like a failure when you make suggestions for a rewrite.

All you need to provide is a place and time to write, materials (pens, crayons, paper), positive encouragement and responses to his work, and praise for his final accomplishment. You might need to provide a few ideas to get the child started, but if you resist the urge to do it for him or rewrite it yourself, your child will enjoy the feeling of responsibility, completion, and ownership of the project.

## STUDY STRATEGIES

There are many strategies to help your child learn more efficiently and effectively. I've personally found the following to be most effective. I've used them academically, professionally, and in my spiritual study life.

- Be sure the child has a sufficient block of time in which to get into the material and concentrate.
- Select an environment in which the child feels comfortable. You may wish to discuss whether music is or is not a distraction and, if it is allowable, what type of music can be played. I personally don't think any type of studying besides simple practice worksheets is possible with the television set on.
- Before beginning to actually study, have the child familiarize herself with the material. Read the back cover or jacket description of the book. Scan the foreword or introduction and the table of contents. Get an idea of what the material is generally going to cover. (When studying books of the Bible, I look at the author, the audience, the time it was written, the key points covered, etc. A study Bible is especially helpful.)
- Next, begin to read through the material with a highlighter pen in hand. (If the school owns the book, a light pencil underline can be used and later erased; but ask the teacher's permission first.) Highlight only the major points and subpoints—key concepts and items that look like they might be on the test (key dates, lists, definitions, etc.).
- Notes can be taken as the child reads through the material or by going back through it afterwards and looking at the highlighted points, depending on how quickly the child is grasping the direction and organization of the piece. A word on note-taking:

Some teachers have specific note-taking methods that must be followed and turned in. They may require complete sentences or simple phrases, outline points to always be multiple (no point A without a point B), a specific outline format, etc. If so, the child should conform to the teacher's requirements. If no such requirements exist, the child is free to develop his own system. The following ideas may help:

I find it easiest to outline in thoughts rather than complete sentences. For instance: a topic (A) followed by subpoints (1, 2, 3). Subsubpoints would be labeled a, b, c, then broken down further into i, ii, iii. The next topic would be B, followed by 1, 2, 3, etc. You can help your child develop a system best suited for the way the particular material is organized.

The child may wish to develop abbreviations for often-used words.

Even the outline can be highlighted to focus on the most important areas.

• After taking notes and highlighting, help the child make herself quiz cards. Just the process of making these cards is very helpful. I have found quiz cards to provide the best way for me to learn.

On one side of an index card, list a key topic, then define it or list major subpoints on the other side. Or list a subpoint as the cue on one side, with subsubpoints on the back. The child can also make up possible test questions and put the answers on the back, or list a date on the front and the significant event that occurred on that date on the back. Use the outline and highlighted material to develop these cards.

Then review the cards backwards and forwards repeatedly (have your child give herself the cue to remember the point, then, vice versa, give herself the major point to remember the cue). After reviewing the cards a couple of times, your child will quickly know many of the answers. Take those cards out of the stack. Keep working by the process of elimination until all cards are memorized. Then start over and work on any cards the child stumbles over.

Be sure your child reviews the cards before going to sleep. The mind continues to "study" while we rest. I would often wake up "caught" on a question and quickly look it up, then never forget it.

Review the cards in the morning and just before the test.

If a cumulative final will be given, save the cards for later study.

Since there is no way to know exactly what questions will be asked on the test, encourage the child to learn *concepts and facts* rather than memorize specific answers to specific questions. These concepts and facts can then be used to construct an answer to an essay question as well.

• Some children find it helpful to study in groups (quiz each other, search for difficult answers, etc.), while others do not. If your child wants to study in a group, make sure they are really studying. When children have good friends who are interested in learning, that interest will help motivate them. However, when they have friends who are not interested in learning, those friends will prove to be a bad influence.

## THE FAMILY'S ROLE

Supportive family members positively impact a child's study skills and academic success. Parents can be a great encouragement and offer practical instruction in specific study skills. You can also help your child evaluate her own achievement or failure and strategize for the future. For instance, if your child does well on an exam, discuss what elements helped her to succeed. How did she study? How did she organize her time and the material? This will reinforce the value of those study skills that she utilized for success. When she does poorly on an exam, discuss how she prepared for the test. How could she have learned the material more effectively? What are some specific study skills she could practice in the future to achieve a higher grade?

What is considered success or failure will differ from child to child. An A student who gets a B because he didn't bother to study has not succeeded at doing his best. On the other hand, a B or C student who studied hard and received a B on the test *has* succeeded in doing his best. We can encourage our children to do their own personal best, no matter what that means in terms of a letter grade. When they fail to do their best, they know it. We can then encourage them to do better next time by helping them find more effective study strategies.

Families can support a student's efforts in many ways, including:

1. Meet excuses with logical reasoning. Explain *why* it is important to study and why the material will be useful to him or her. Instead of saying "Just do it," help the child see the importance.
2. Enforce house rules on studying. If the television is not allowed on during study time, turn it off. If you find it turned on again, remove it from the room. Allow the child to control the environment and decide when to study *only as long as* he or she is doing so responsibly.
3. Help use time management skills to balance sports, lessons, and playtime with homework.
4. Help the child plan ahead to study for tests and complete assignments on time without last-minute pressure.
5. Set priorities, such as no television until homework is completed.

6. Most children require an average of two hours of homework a night to get their best grades.
7. Siblings should quietly respect the study environment (no interrupting or playing a loud stereo in the next room).
8. Teach your children that if they have good study skills and no distractions, it will cut their study time in half!

## Bringing It Home

*Applying God's Principles: Please refer to Chapter 2 for ideas on Family Night format and activities.*

**Opening:** Why is hard work valuable? What kinds of things would you describe as hard work?

**Scripture:** Proverbs 20:4; 2 Timothy 2:15; 2 Thessalonians 3:10; Colossians 3:23.

**Discussion:** What does God say about those who work hard? What happens to those who don't work? What if you don't *like* the work you are doing or the person for whom you work?

**Application:** Read the following example:

John and Dave both work for the Sport Clothes Shop. John works eight hours a day and gets all of his work done. When he finishes stocking the shelves, he waits for the boss to give him another task. Dave also works eight hours a day and gets all of his work done. When he finishes stocking the shelves, he looks around to see what else needs to be done. He works on pricing some shirts. When someone needs to stay late after work to help, Dave volunteers. A new position opens up. The boss has to decide whether the promotion and raise should go to Dave or John.

1. If you were the boss, to whom would you give the promotion and raise? Why?

2. Are you more like Dave or John?

3. Each person should choose an area in which they'd like to work a little harder. What are some practical ways to be more efficient?

# CONCLUSION

◆

When our children encounter temptation, we pray they will make godly, moral decisions. It all begins with us—the parents. As we pour our efforts into modeling a Christian lifestyle and teaching our children as we discipline them, we are helping to build the character of our children as we ourselves grow.

The biblical principles outlined in this book can help each of us—each member of our families—to live successfully for the Lord. As we obey and follow the Word, our guide for life, we will benefit in every area of our lives and will better understand how to protect and nurture our children.

Despite the negative influences and ungodly philosophies our children encounter in public schools and society, we can help them to achieve and use their God-given abilities for His glory.

If we follow God's plan for training our children (rather than the worldly plan promoted by well-intentioned psychologists), we can put them on auto-pilot and rest assured that we've done our very best to encourage our children to make godly choices and live successful lives. The earlier we begin biblical training, the more effective our efforts will be. But never give up—it's never too late!

Remember, we do our best but must never take setbacks too seriously. We'll always have difficulties in some areas, but that doesn't make us failures as parents. The Lord knows our hearts, and He will bless our sincere efforts.

No area of parenting is easy, but every area can be made fun. By teaching, modeling, encouraging, praying for, discipling, and overall training your children, you will help them avoid the negative temptations of this world and will give them the greatest gift of all—success at living a godly Christian lifestyle that reaps eternal rewards!

Every family can achieve success. So keep on trying; you'll be glad you did, on that final day when you hear the Lord say, "Well done, good and faithful servant." I pray that the Lord will be with you as you obey Him in implementing these training principles.

God bless you!

# SCRIPTURE INDEX

# GENERAL INDEX

To obtain the materials published by Citizens for Excellence in Education and mentioned in this book, write CEE at P.O. Box 3200, Costa Mesa, CA 92628 or call (714) 251-9333.